STRIKE A BLOW AND DIE ●

Center for International Affairs, Harvard University

STRIKE A BLOW AND DIE ●

A Narrative of Race Relations in Colonial
Africa by George Simeon Mwase

EDITED AND INTRODUCED BY ROBERT I. ROTBERG

Harvard University Press · Cambridge, Massachusetts · 1967

28432C

EDITOR'S ACKNOWLEDGMENTS

Although the present book is a natural outgrowth of my previous work on the history of Malawi, its editing occasioned a fresh study of the Chilembwe rebellion of 1915, the life and times of George Mwase, and the many subjects in which he demonstrated an interest. Once again Professor George Shepperson generously allowed me to draw upon his own vast knowledge of the period portrayed by Mwase. Mr. Ian Nance, who knew Mwase during the 1940's and 1950's, responded fully to my numerous requests for assistance over the course of several years. I profited much from his penetrating criticism of the introduction and edited text that follow. Dr. Jaap van Velsen kindly scrutinized the proofs and provided new information about Mwase's life. Mr. Maurice Gandy and Mr. Goodnews Mwase (Mwase's son) provided biographical information. The Rev. Mr. Andrew Ross and Mr. Anthony Wilson kindly made inquiries when I could not. Mr. Thomas Nighswander likewise uncovered material about Mwase for me in Nkhata Bay and Professor Erich Gruen assisted me with translations from Latin.

I am especially indebted to Messrs. Goodnews and Simeon Mwase for their cooperation in the publication of their father's book.

I am also grateful to the Center for International Affairs for facilitating the preparation of the volume. In the cheerfully efficient manner on which I have often relied, Mrs. Jane French Tatlock transformed my own typescript into one that others could read. Joanna, my wife, wisely criticized and appropriately amended many of the crucial editorial decisions.

Robert I. Rotberg

Harvard University
14 July 1965
7 December 1966

CONTENTS

Contents

INTRODUCTION BY ROBERT I. ROTBERG

The African narrative here published for the first time had lain in the archives of Nyasaland (now Malawi) for nearly thirty years, apparently unnoticed, until my wife and I discovered it in the course of research there in 1962. A typescript, it bore the title "A Dialogue of Nyasaland Record of Past Events, Environments & the Present Outlook within the Protectorate." The author's name was George S. Mwase.

We already knew that George Simeon Mwase, who had died a few weeks before, had long been regarded by many white administrators as an excessively opinionated, "harmless," compulsive writer of memoranda and tracts. He may have hoped to become regarded as a latter-day William Prynne, but the Government of Nyasaland had always replied to his missives in the noncommittal, routine manner it reserved for cranks and other meddlesome Africans. At first we discounted the conceivable importance of the "Dialogue" and consigned it in our order of priorities to the category of material that might be looked at later— if there were "time." Some days after the "Dialogue" first came to our attention, however, a cursory reading of the typescript quickly established its very great historical and sociological value.

Foremost, the "Dialogue" contains the only lengthy African biography of John Chilembwe (d. 1915), Nyasaland's first revolutionary. It also includes a perceptive analysis of the Nyasa rebellion of 1915 and adds hitherto unknown detail to our knowledge of its origins and participants. Finally, the "Dialogue" contains a personal commentary upon race relations and the conditions of indigenous life in Nyasaland during the early 1930's, when Mwase—at various times a government clerk, storekeeper, and politician—composed his manuscript. It should be read with all those divers qualities in mind.

Mwase's book is not a "dialogue" in the ordinary sense, and for that reason and for the sake of clarity I have taken the liberty of supplying it with a more appropriate title from his own text—*Strike a Blow and Die.* Additional editorial decisions are explained in the "Note on the Text and the Editing," which precedes his narrative.

THE HISTORICAL SETTING

By the beginning of the twentieth century, all of the peoples who lived along the western and southern marches of Lake Nyasa had, after submitting to the importunities and aggressions of aliens, lost their independence and commenced to experience the realities of British rule. The process of change had begun about sixty years before when Ngoni warriors, fleeing originally from Zululand, had disturbed the prevailing atmosphere of apparent calm and had annexed and settled among sections of the Malawi and associated peoples who hitherto had controlled the approaches to the lake. Between 1859 and 1863 David Livingstone had explored the area. Scottish missionaries commemorated his exploits by settling both to the south of the lake, in the Shire Highlands, and to the west, among the Tonga and Ngoni tribes. They took the gospel of Christ in its Western garb to peoples comparatively unacquainted with nineteenth-century ideological and technological notions of progress. They also set in motion a series of imperial events that ultimately resulted in British conquest.

Although the missionaries provided an essential excuse, the "scramble for Africa" and the specific threat of a Portuguese invasion precipitated British diplomatic and military maneuvers in 1889 and 1890 that placed the Malawi, Ngoni, Tonga, and other lacustrine peoples firmly within the British sphere of influence. In 1891, Britain officially "protected" these peoples and inaugurated what was known until 1964 as Nyasaland.[1] This protection, although based ostensibly upon a number of hastily collected expressions of friendship that Britons called "treaties," derived its functional legitimacy from the repeated demonstration of British power rather than from any self-interested devolution of sovereignty by Africans. Throughout the early 1890's, British troops engaged in a succession of military campaigns against those Yao, Ngoni, and Cewa chiefs who chose forcibly and, in the end, forlornly to oppose the imposition of British overrule. Later, these newly protected peoples and the others who, understanding the message of might, had refrained from displays of antagonism, began to participate—at first hesitantly and ambivalently—in the political and material transformation of their homeland.[2]

1. Originally the Nyasaland Districts Protectorate, and between 1893 and 1907 the British Central Africa Protectorate, it was thereafter called the Protectorate of Nyasaland.

2. The argument contained in this introduction follows that set out at greater length and documented in the opening chapters of Robert I. Rotberg, *The Rise of Nationalism in Central Africa: The Making of Malawi and Zambia 1873–1964* (Cambridge, Mass.: Harvard University Press, 1965).

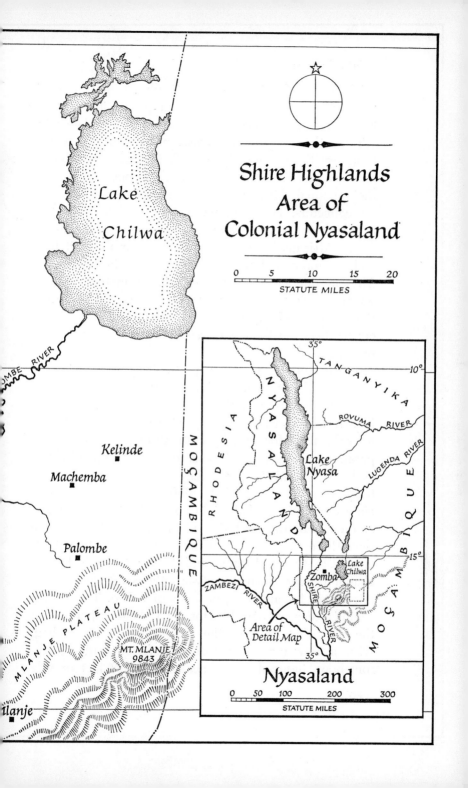

Lake
Chilwa

Shire Highlands
Area of
Colonial Nyasaland

0   5   10   15   20
STATUTE MILES

OMBE RIVER

Kelinde

Machemba

Palombe

M L A N J E   P L A T E A U

MT. MLANJE
9843

Mlanje

MOÇAMBIQUE

35°

T A N G A N Y I K A   10°

RHODESIA

N Y A S A L A N D

ROVUMA RIVER

Lake
Nyasa

LUGENDA RIVER

M O Ç A M B I Q U E

15°

ZAMBEZI RIVER

SHIRE RIVER

Zomba

Lake
Chilwa

Area of
Detail Map

35°

Nyasaland

0   50   100   200   300
STATUTE MILES

Introduction

The onset of British rule drastically altered the traditional way of life. Deprived of a proportion of their lands and encouraged by various means to labor for whites, the peoples of Nyasaland reluctantly began to accept the ukase of British officialdom and to forfeit a large part of their earnings, their possessions, and their manual skills in order to satisfy the demands of tax collectors. They also came to appreciate the extent to which white men thought dark-skinned peoples inferior; Africans knew color prejudice for the first time and, as more and more whites settled in Nyasaland, Africans increasingly suffered discrimination. Everywhere, during the opening decades of this century, the peoples of Nyasaland found their freedom circumscribed and their lives regulated according to alien precepts.

These conditions grew particularly acute in the Shire Highlands, where whites settled in number during the 1890's. With the encouragement of the local British administration, many of these settlers hoped to make their fortunes by cultivating the fertile, comparatively well-watered soils of the Highlands. Together with missionaries, they quickly acquired vast tracts of land from tribal chiefs who did not appreciate the value of their rights or understand the effect of their actions. Chief Kapeni of the Yao "sold" more than three thousand acres for a gun, thirty-two yards of calico, two red caps, and "other things"; he exchanged more than twenty-six thousand acres to a missionary for about 1,750 yards of calico. The British commissioner responsible for Nyasaland explained at the time that most of the would-be purchasers had, with a few pounds' worth of inferior trade goods, somehow "induced some heedless young Chief or silly old savage to put his mark on a paper conferring vast territories and sovereign rights. . . ." [3]

A local white judge decided that chiefs as a class had illegally "sold" their lands. Chiefs were not, he said, custodians of their tribal lands. They had no right, even with the consent of their people, to dispose of freehold rights or grant easements.[4] Nevertheless, more than half of the most suitable acreage in the densely populated Shire Highlands remained in white ownership. (Over-all, about fifteen per cent of the entire land and water area of the Protectorate passed into the settler-controlled domain.) Within this alienated portion of the Highlands—much of which remained underdeveloped—Africans, although theoretically privileged, experienced all of the unexpected discomforts of landless tenants. Africans had lost what agricultural peoples always prize most—unhindered access to arable land and the right to use such land in a manner sanctified by tradition. The same judge compared conditions in Nyasaland with conditions in mediaeval Europe: the African tended, he said, "to differ in one respect from the mediaeval villein. If the latter were bound to the soil he had at least a fixity of tenure. The native, apparently, is to have eventually no tenure at all." The judge went on to catalogue many of the consequences of the wholesale alienation of African land:

The natives, in return for a past consideration—the fact that they have been allowed to change their gardens at some

3. Foreign Office 84/2197: H. H. Johnston to Lord Rosebery, 13 October 1892, quoted in Roland Oliver, *Sir Harry Johnston and the Scramble for Africa* (London, 1957), 220–221.
4. Judge John Joseph Nunan, judgment in Supervisor of Native Affairs *v.* Blantyre and East Africa Company, Blantyre, 28 April 1903, Zomba archives.

date not mentioned—surrender a freehold, or claim of freehold, and receive a tenancy at will, with the s[u]peradded condition that if they do not work for the land-owner . . . for two months . . . during the rainy season (a period at which their labour is particularly valuable to themselves, as it includes two out of the three months of their own hoeing time), they are bound to pay 6s. annual rent . . . an annual payment equivalent to 120 per cent of the fee simple. The native has no security of tenure, must move without compensation when called upon . . . and can take up no fresh ground for his garden [without] permission. It is to this that British protection has brought the Central African native. . . .[5]

Planters, complained an important administrator, simply wanted cheap labor and disliked policies that tended to raise the natives above the level "at which they would be content to work for him at a pittance."[6] As a result, the lack of rights of landless Africans remained a source of grievance and controversy throughout the colonial period. By the 1920's, Africans who resided upon white-owned plantations in the Highlands had the option of either working there, paying a cash rental, or subjecting themselves to eviction and the long, rather difficult process of finding new plots on which to plant subsistence crops. If they remained tenants, whites told them what and when they should and could cultivate and, at arbitrarily contrived prices, purchased the resultant crops in lieu of rent. White managers refused to allow their tenants to grow maize and other foodstuffs for personal profit. They prevented Africans from cutting down trees in order to build huts in the customary manner. In an area where the

5. *Ibid.*
6. Colonial Office 525/49: Deputy Governor Francis Barrow Pearce to the Secretary of State for the Colonies, 14 June 1913, Public Record Office, London.

accepted pattern of residence was matrilocal, whites denied young men the opportunity to live with their prospective in-laws. Although whites viewed these and a number of other constraints as logical and even necessary exercises in defense of private property, Africans considered them harsh and irrational abuses. An African who regarded whites and the coming of white rule with suspicion could have his worst fears confirmed by becoming a tenant upon a white-owned plantation.

From the early 1890's, the government of Nyasaland taxed Africans in the Shire Highlands in order to encourage them to work for whites and contribute to the costs of their own "protection." From 1892, administrators assessed each adult male at three shillings multiplied by the number of huts he "owned" (a man had to maintain a separate dwelling for each of his wives). Meanwhile, wages throughout the Protectorate were set at a monthly level corresponding to the individual's annual tax obligation; accordingly, if an African had three wives, whites expected him to work for three additional months merely in order to fulfill his obligations to the collector of taxes.

Initially, this manipulation of the laws of supply and demand and the absence of serious competition sufficed to supply administrators, missionaries, and planters with labor in reasonable abundance. But as the settler population increased and the coffee industry grew, the demand for porters, household servants, road workers, and field hands intensified correspondingly. To the annoyance of the tax, the government of Nyasaland therefore added the bitter burden of compulsion. A plentiful supply of labor—despite the opposition of the British Foreign and Colonial Offices—became dependent partially upon the "moral influence" exercised by white administrators over Africans. One official in 1906 supposed that "many thousands of natives, by a judicious admixture of authority and persuasion [had been] induced to bestir themselves [perhaps] against their immediate inclinations. . . ." [7]

Such policies provided planters with labor during the first four decades of the twentieth century. The rate of taxation increased; in 1902, the administration doubled it, although simultaneously offering a fifty per cent rebate to Africans who worked for Europeans for at least one month each year. In 1920, the rebate was withdrawn. In 1927, the rate went up again to nine shillings per hut. Revenues increased commensurately and, by such means, Africans contributed significantly—proportionally more than they received in return—to the recurrent costs of the administration of the Protectorate. No figures are available for the interwar period, but in 1913 more than one million Africans were said to supply about seventy per cent of the annual revenue of the Protectorate. They also produced the crops grown by Nyasaland's approximately one hundred planters, and made life more comfortable for the approximately two hundred missionaries and one hundred administrators who had effectively also become their masters. [8]

The impressment of labor in lieu of taxes had always helped to satisfy some of the economic needs of the Protectorate. In the 1920's, after raising the rates of taxation, the Government of Nyasaland also improved its methods of dealing punitively with de-

7. Hector Livingston Duff, *Nyasaland Under the Foreign Office* (London, 1906), 355–356.
8. GOA 5/3/1: Francis Barrow Peace's "confidential notes," August 1913, Zomba archives.

faulters. Sometimes administrators burned the huts
of defaulters; sometimes they seized their wives. In
1921, the Government of Nyasaland officially recog-
nized the necessity of taking hostages; seven years
later senior members of the administration approved
the demolition of the huts of adult male defaulters
and "the huts of women whose husbands are in Southern Rhodesia and who have not paid the hut tax. . . ."
"I would add," the Chief Secretary wrote, "that the
simplest way of destroying a hut is to have it de-
molished with poles. . . . If you burn and a wind
gets up other huts are apt to catch fire." [9]

A government that seemed to devote nearly all of
its energy to the collection of taxes and the punishment of defaulters was unlikely to arouse African ac-
claim. Although it made roads and began the long
process of opening up the territory, the government,
aside from encouraging the efforts of missionaries, had,
by 1920, done little to eradicate or cure disease or
to educate Africans. It had destroyed much traditional tribal authority without providing a replace-
ment. Moreover, whites had erected an extralegal but
nonetheless effective color bar that, together with the
ever-present atmosphere of prejudice, daily forced Africans to taste inferiority and savor their own humiliation.

"The government apparently does nothing for the
natives," a missionary complained. "In the whole of
Central Angoniland there is not a single Government
doctor or hospital, and the Government contribution
to mission societies for education is practically nil.
. . . Government does bring peace to Africans, but

9. S 1/312/21: the Chief Secretary, circular letter, 24 October
1921; the Chief Secretary to C. J. Brackenbury, provincial commissioner, 16 March 1928, Zomba archives.

they say there used to be long intervals of peace in the old days. Now their obligations are never ending: they labour for the government, they pay a yearly tax, they are bullied by *askaris* [soldiers]. They conclude that they are now practically all *akapolo,* or slaves, whereas the slave raiders, of whom the government has freed them, always left the great majority free." [10]

THE CHILEMBWE REBELLION

It is of those conditions that George Simeon Mwase wrote. They provide the historical setting for the bulk of his book. They also enable the reader to appreciate many of the social factors that formed the causal underpinning of the Chilembwe rebellion which Mwase discusses at length. John Chilembwe, whose biographer Mwase became, was born, c. 1860–1871, in the Shire Highlands. He attended a Church of Scotland mission school in Blantyre and, in 1892, attached himself to Joseph Booth, a fervently evangelical British fundamentalist visionary who had opened his own Baptist mission near Blantyre. For several years Chilembwe imbibed Booth's heady egalitarian brew. Then, together, they traveled to the United States, where Booth found Chilembwe a place in a Negro Baptist seminary in Virginia. There, particularly within the American Negro circles that he penetrated, Chilembwe's growing independence of mind and attitude of racial assertiveness found fresh support. There, too, he probably learned of the Negro's revolutionary heritage, and,

10. D. K. van Oesterzee, of the Dedza Dutch Reformed Church Mission, *The Nyasaland Times,* 17 March 1921.

apparently, of the abolitionist John Brown and his raid upon Harpers Ferry in 1859.

When Chilembwe returned to Nyasaland in 1900, he came with evangelical ends in mind. Supported financially by the National Baptist Convention of the United States, a Negro organization, he obtained land near Mbombwe in the Chiradzulu district and opened the first and only station of what he called the Providence Industrial Mission. Before many years had passed, the mission had gained adherents throughout the Shire Highlands and in neighboring Moçambique. Chilembwe established a chain of independent African schools, erected an impressive brick church, and planted crops of coffee, cotton, and tea.

Throughout the years before 1914, officials and missionaries regarded Chilembwe with favor. Mwase comments at length about his deportment and explains why he was so widely respected. Apparently no one in authority viewed Chilembwe as a subversive citizen; for the most part, before 1914, he busied himself with the affairs of his mission and his schools, a store in which he had an interest, and the Natives' Industrial Union—an embryo Chamber of Commerce. Unlike Elliot Kenan Kamwana Achirwa, he eschewed millenarianism and, as far as we know, disseminated orthodox Baptist teachings.

What transformed Chilembwe from an independent-minded evangelist into the first revolutionary in colonial eastern and central Africa? Mwase, in company with George Shepperson and Thomas Price, the authors of *Independent African: John Chilembwe and the Origins, Setting and Significance of the Nyasaland Native Rising of 1915* (Edinburgh, 1958), emphasizes the various social causes to which this introduction has already alluded. He mentions the atmosphere of discontent that then pervaded the Shire Highlands; nowhere was this atmosphere more oppressive than upon the vast estate that belonged to A. Livingstone Bruce, was managed by William Jervis Livingstone, and bordered Chilembwe's Providence mission at Mbombwe. William Livingstone, who was unrelated to the explorer, dealt harshly with his tenants and laborers and, as Mwase indicates, burned the churches that Chilembwe's followers had erected upon the estate. Conditions of employment there, even by the standards of the neighborhood, were particularly bad.

Again in accord with Shepperson and Price, who did not know of Mwase's text when they wrote their own biography,[11] Mwase indicates that Chilembwe particularly grieved for those Nyasas who had died fighting the white men's wars—"which war[s]," Mwase wrote, "was nothing to do with them." [12] Finally, the outbreak of World War I and the immediate involvement of Nyasas in the Anglo-German confrontation in East and Central Africa set alight the tinder of dismay that had long flickered in Chilembwe's soul. The loss of African lives in the battle of Karonga, and the prospect of continued deaths if the war proved lengthy, confirmed him in his opposition to colonial rule.

Mwase provides the first comparatively detailed

11. Shepperson and Price in *Independent African*, however, used an unpublished narrative (c. 1951) composed by Andrew G. Mkulichi, one of Chilembwe's followers. Mkulichi may just conceivably have had access to Mwase's earlier typescript. Or Mwase, years before, may have derived some of his information from Mkulichi, who in turn subsequently wrote it up. Or the two narratives may simply represent the conjunction of separately received oral traditions.

12. Mwase (in the present book), 32–33

account of the conspiracy that rapidly moved toward revolt after Chilembwe had failed to obtain satisfaction by stating his grievances in writing. According to Mwase, whose analysis of the rebellion is too detailed and too susceptible of elaborate corroboration to have been manufactured, Chilembwe and his followers (precise numbers are never specified) met several times in December 1914, and then, in early January 1915, finally decided to "strike a blow and die," for then "our blood will surely mean something at last." [13] The moving refrain of Mwase's account of the prelude to conflict, *"Let us strike a blow and die,"* emphasized the essentially symbolic intent of the rebellion. If we accept the implications of Mwase's narrative, Chilembwe intended the rebellion to demonstrate the depth of African discontent rather than to precipitate a revolution that would oust colonial rule. Such a conclusion would help to explain why Chilembwe enrolled so few Africans in his cause (Mwase implies that the army numbered less than a hundred) and why so few white-owned estates and white facilities were attacked. It cannot necessarily account, however, for Chilembwe's rather maladroit attempt to enlist the sympathies of the German regime in East Africa,[14] his attempt to sponsor a secondary rising in the Ncheu district, the cutting of telegraph lines by his followers, or his own flight.

Chilembwe's decision to demonstrate discontent, to "strike a blow and die," was in the spirit of radical Christian revolt. More specifically—and Mwase sub-

13. Mwase, 36.
14. Robert I. Rotberg, "Resistance and Rebellion in British Nyasaland and German East Africa, 1888–1915," in *Britain and Germany in Africa,* ed. Prosser Gifford and William Roger Louis (New Haven, 1967), 688–689.

stantiates in detail a suspicion adumbrated by Shepperson and Price[15]—Chilembwe derived either his inspiration or the logic of his decision from his own acquaintance with or perhaps vague recollection of the myth of John Brown. The hagiolatrous presentation of Brown's life and deeds in American Negro circles had, during Chilembwe's lifetime, surrounded the raid on Harpers Ferry with much more of an aura of accomplishment than, in the balanced view, it now possesses. According to Mwase, for Chilembwe the proposed Nyasa rebellion stood "the same as that of a Mr. John Brown." [16]

Although conclusive evidence is lacking, the editor surmises that Chilembwe's knowledge of the life and deeds of John Brown was derived from the pages of Frederick Douglass' autobiography. Douglass, who had been an American slave, published his final, completely revised version in 1892, the same year when Chilembwe became associated with Joseph Booth and a few years before Chilembwe and Booth arrived in America. An analysis of John Brown, a central figure in Douglass' life, occupies sizable portions of the second part of the autobiography. Douglass dissects Brown's character, motives, and strategy in a way that may well have appealed to Chilembwe. Finally Douglass, referring to a conversation he had with Brown before the raid on Harpers Ferry, uses the very form of words that—if Mwase is to be believed—became the *leitmotiv* of the rebellion: "Our talk was long and earnest; we spent the most of a Saturday and a part of Sunday in this debate—Brown for Harpers Ferry, and I against it—he for striking a blow which should

15. *Independent African*, 239.
16. Mwase, 36.

John Chilembwe and family, about ten years before the 1915 rebellion

Mwase in 1961 with son Goodnews Mwase (right) and two grandchildren

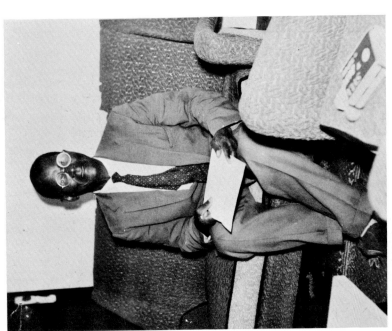

George Simeon Mwase in 1960

instantly rouse the country, and I for the policy of gradually and unaccountably drawing off the slaves to the mountains, as at first suggested and proposed by him." [17]

Presumably, regardless of how Chilembwe learned about John Brown, he consciously chose to don the same mantle of martyrdom that he assumed that Brown had worn. It would have been easy for Chilembwe to have assumed further, albeit erroneously, that Brown's raid had by itself provoked the American Civil War —a war that Chilembwe (despite his sojourn in the American South) perhaps saw simply as a victory for the Negrophile forces of freedom. When the outbreak of World War I and the government's failure to heed his cry plunged him from the plains of indecision into the chasm of conspiracy, Chilembwe may well have imagined that it was his duty to emulate Brown and to seek a parallel martyrdom in order to free his own people from bondage.

Mwase's account of the preparations for and the events of the rising (which again agrees substantially with, and supplements, that contained in the growing literature of the period) bears out such a hypothesis. He quotes at length a speech that Chilembwe supposedly delivered to his army immediately before ordering them into battle on 23 January 1915. (Precisely why Chilembwe and his followers rose on that particular day remains obscure.) "You are all patriots," Chilembwe said, and "this very night you are to go

17. *Life and Times of Frederick Douglass: His Early Life as a Slave, His Escape from Bondage, and His Complete History* (New York: 1962 edition), 319–320. Other passages on John Brown are at 273–275, 303–307, and 314–319. This is a reprinting of the 1892 edition. Sections of the autobiography were published in 1845 and 1855, the first complete edition in 1881.

and strike the blow and then die. I do not say that you are going to win the war at all." He encouraged his hearers to do it for the love of their country and countrymen. He said that this was the only way to show the white men "that the treatment they are treating our men and women was most bad," and that they might change for the better "after we are dead and buried." [18] It is known that he cautioned his followers—contrary to what the Government of Nyasaland later assumed—to eschew any idea that they might overthrow the government and rule in its stead. He directed them not to molest white women and children, to refrain from looting, and to signify their gesture of protest by cutting off the heads of one or more planters. And throughout the hours of the short-lived rebellion, Chilembwe made his headquarters, meditated, and conceivably readied himself for martyrdom atop Chilimangwanje Hill near Mbombwe.

We can now reconstruct the course of the rising with fair accuracy. The rebels faithfully observed Chilembwe's instructions. One group attacked the Bruce estate, killed three planters, cut off the head of William Jervis Livingstone and returned with it to Mbombwe, and preserved several white women and children from harm. They took guns and ammunition, but refrained from firing crops or houses or otherwise damaging the estate. At the same time, their compatriots failed in an attempt to raid small arsenals in Blantyre and in the Chiradzulu *boma* (or administrative headquarters), and a forewarned official arrested the followers of Filipo Chinyama before they could attack the *boma* at Ncheu. Mwase indicates that a number of other participants "shrinked" from their appointed

18. Mwase, 48–49.

tasks, which included attacks on other planters in Nsoni, Mlanje, and Zomba, and a foray into Limbe. *Askari* in Blantyre had also reneged on a promise to participate. Confusing and, if true, apparently destructive of the hypothesis already advanced, is Mwase's further hint that Chilembwe had originally hoped that Chinyama, after succeeding in Ncheu, would lead his fellow rebels southward to Liwonde, Neno, and Blantyre, where they would link up with the main force, and, presumably, attempt to conquer Blantyre. But, as yet, this brief section of Mwase's narrative is particularly difficult to interpret and substantiate. Most of the available evidence points to an opposite conclusion.

The revolt soon collapsed. After the feverish activity of the first evening, the rebels forfeited their advantage of surprise and remained on the defensive. Except for a conceivably unpremeditated attack upon a Roman Catholic mission station, Chilembwe's men made no new raids, fought a desultory rearguard action against the advancing white militia, and apparently accepted the essence of their failure and probable fate with passive resignation. When all seemed lost, Chilembwe and many of his accomplices fled toward Moçambique. Ten days later, an African policeman shot Chilembwe near Kelinde, north of Mlanje; other rebels were captured, tried, and hanged or imprisoned.

In the immediate context, Chilembwe and his followers accomplished little. Their actions largely failed to improve the lot of their countrymen. Indeed, whites were unable to appreciate the sense of the cautionary tale and, instead, made of every subsequent manifestation of discontent the dangerous conspiracy of revolt. When they remembered Chilembwe at all, whites reviled his memory; but Africans revered him as the most important of their early patriots. Mwase, emphasizing the importance of charisma (without using the term), likens Chilembwe to a man who intrepidly attacks a lion armed only with a maize stalk. As John Brown's deeds were celebrated in song, so Mwase believed that Chilembwe's actions would always be commemorated by his countrymen.

The merit of Mwase's book lies largely in his analysis of Chilembwe's actions and the narration of the events of the rising. Essentially, Mwase relates received tradition and summarizes events as they were made known to him. Selected episodes, therefore, receive particular attention; matters of which Mwase had learned much are set out at length, and the result is hardly a balanced account. With Chilembwe firmly in the foreground, the narrative proceeds, with occasional fits and starts, along an essentially chronological path of rebellion until, before Mwase examines in detail the motives of the chief protagonist, he pauses to follow two tangential trails.

Along one, Mwase speculates about what he considers Chilembwe's rather odd decision to seek support from the Germans. In passing, Mwase indicates that he personally had some acquaintance with the German administration in East Africa, and he compares it unfavorably to the British administration of Nyasaland.

Along the other bypath Mwase follows the flight of Wallace Kampingo—the only one of Chilembwe's lieutenants that he singles out for such careful attention—after the collapse of the revolt. In themselves the particular events are interesting only for connoisseurs of the period. But their inclusion in Mwase's book may answer perplexing questions about the sources of Mwase's information. Given his own silence —Mwase was not known for his modesty—and the likelihood that he then worked in Northern Rhodesia, it is clear that Mwase himself did not participate in the rising. His home was far away, and nearly all of the participants in the rising were affiliated to tribes of the Shire Highlands. He might, as a some-time government clerk, have later possessed access to documents that are now lost (much of his detail is unduplicated in the Zomba archives), but, if so, there seems no good reason why he would have re-frained from mentioning his sources. He may have had a number of informants, but only Kampingo could have related so thoroughly the events of his own escape and final arrest. Furthermore, Kampingo was an inmate of the Zomba Central Prison when Mwase arrived there in 1931. Kampingo was released on 2 July 1932. Mwase was released about two weeks later. Kampingo had served seventeen years of a life sentence that he had received for taking part in the Chilembwe rebellion. In prison, Kampingo was employed as a ward orderly in the prison hospital, where Mwase spent some months.[19] Kampingo is almost certainly the "eyewitness" to whom Mwase refers in the opening paragraphs of the "Dia-logue."

RACE RELATIONS, PENOLOGY, AND LAW

The last five chapters of the book are pure Mwase. They express often idiosyncratic but always interest-ing views upon the colonial history of Nyasaland and

19. For the information about Kampingo in prison, the editor is indebted to D. E. Creasey, Acting Superintendent, Zomba Central Prison, letter of 10 August 1965.

the contemporary scene in about 1932. In one chapter Mwase contrasts the bad old days, when planters ruled arbitrarily and compulsory labor was in vogue, with the favorable new dispensation. Surprisingly—in view of the mass of evidence to the contrary and his own subsequent statements [20]—he avers that race relations had improved significantly, that "a whiteman is a friend of a native all round," [21] that Africans occupied positions previously reserved for whites (Levi Mumba, the first African to occupy an appointive office, was not appointed to the Native Education Board until 1933), and that whites listened attentively to the raised voices of Africans. He further reported that administrators no longer seized the wives of tax defaulters. He praised the caliber of the white planting community and condoned the abuses to which tenants on alienated estates remained subject. But his review varies so greatly from the norm of other contemporary accounts and archival evidence that Mwase either must have been leading a sheltered life or wanted to accentuate the positive aspects of his surroundings in order to dramatize such improvements as there undoubtedly were—or, as an ex-prisoner, hoped to curry the favor of officials.

Most Africans reviled Asians. They occupied the interstices in the social grid that, the world over, are reserved for petty traders. Discriminated against by whites, they nevertheless—in terms of the European scale of values (which Asians and Africans largely internalized)—occupied an intermediate rank significantly above that designated for Africans and slightly above that station to which "coloureds," that is, mulattoes, were assigned. Asians in turn naturally discrim-

20. See Rotberg, *Rise of Nationalism,* chaps. 2–6.
21. Mwase, 84.

inated against their supposed inferiors. They also developed a reputation for being unscrupulous, usurious, and spineless. But Mwase came to their defense. He argued that Asian shopkeepers did not discriminate against Africans as viciously as whites did. The Asian businessman, he wrote, felt sympathy for Africans. Mwase, who had earlier operated his own rural store in competition with Indians, reported that Asians regularly gave credit to Africans.

In company with many educated Africans, Mwase was concerned with the coloured problem. Since the earliest penetration of Europeans into the Nyasa region, whites and Africans had cohabited and produced children of mixed blood. Before the settler frontier had embraced Nyasaland, these liaisons often constituted common-law marriage and the children grew up in a familial surrounding. But the arrival of white women, and the strength of Victorian and Edwardian *mores*, ended the general acceptance of common-law unions across supposed racial barriers. As these arrangements tended to become more fugitive and often adulterous, the children suffered. Mwase complains that African mothers were unable to bring up coloured children properly in the villages. He wanted whites to acknowledge their illegitimate coloured offspring and to incorporate them into their own households with or without the African mothers. Despite the efforts of Mwase and his contemporaries, however, whites continued to evade their responsibilities, and the mulatto problem remained a source of constant African embarrassment and humiliation.

Few Africans have ever written about penology. Mwase, who had considerable experience, takes great pains to dispel African fears of prison conditions. For a man recently released or, conceivably, still serving his sentence, Mwase lavishes surprising praise upon many aspects of penal life. In his day, convicts serving time in the Central Prison in Zomba received what he describes as excellent medical care, good food, and fair treatment. Warders flogged only those who deserved it, although prisoners in outlying centers were often beaten without cause. Mwase notes but does not object to rules against smoking and against conversation, and the general atmosphere of regimentation. Although he suggests several minor reforms, Mwase's general presentation of prison life is favorable to the authorities. His report contrasts sharply with other African views.[22] Was he ingenuous, or can he have again hoped to ingratiate himself with the white rulers?

In his last chapter, Mwase considers various aspects of the white man's legal system. After urging the government to punish adultery among Africans more severely in accord with customary law, he devotes the remainder of his pages to an all-out attack upon regulations that prevented Africans from indiscriminately denuding the forests and catchment basins of the Shire Highlands and limited the number and kinds of game animals that they could kill. The concept of conservation puzzled Africans; heretofore, trees to burn and with which to construct dwellings had never seemed in short supply, and game, which they shot for the pot rather than for purposes of sport or subsequent display, had been relatively abundant. Whites nonetheless said that they desired to preserve wood-

22. In 1936, on behalf of the Zomba Native Civil Servants Association, Levi Mumba complained in strong terms to the Government about the treatment received by African prisoners. NC 1/3/6: Levi Mumba to the Senior Provincial Commissioner, 14 March 1936, Zomba archives.

land areas for the benefit of future generations and would limit the shooting of animals to the extent of their natural increase. Africans, well-represented by Mwase, looked askance at such legislation. They surmised that the white-run government merely wanted to keep the trees and the game to themselves, and that conservation laws were designed—along with so many other regulations—to deprive Africans of their natural rights. Throughout the colonial period such generally unenforceable laws invited wholesale evasion. During the nationalistic period of the 1950's, similarly intended agricultural rules even served as foci for the violent expression of indigenous discontent.

Mwase wrote the following narrative initially in order to acquaint his countrymen with the true story of the patriot John Chilembwe. His urge to put pen to paper was no doubt stimulated by the meeting in prison with Wallace Kampingo. Since the first and second halves of Mwase's book are so dissimilar in subject matter, it is perhaps proper to believe that Mwase set his thoughts down over a relatively long period of months, both in and out of prison. It is equally possible that he simply felt the need to produce a book-length manuscript and therefore to supplement the discussion of Chilembwe with a number of pertinent observations, or the latter may—positive external or internal evidence is unavailable—represent a series of separately written essays, subsequently collected. In any event, all of the chapters bear the unmistakable imprint of Mwase's mind. Sometimes he is naive or fanciful. Contradictions of substance there are, but the importance of his discussion of Chilembwe, with its body of new data and suggestions for further research, and the freshness of his divers concluding essays are unquestionable. Mwase's "Dialogue" reflects both the age in which it was written and the concerns of a member of the indigenous intelligentsia. It is valuable on those grounds alone. It also represents the only detailed political, historical, or sociological treatise written by a Nyasa resident in Nyasaland before World War II. It sharpens our awareness of the roots and development of Nyasa self-assertion.

MWASE: A BIOGRAPHICAL NOTE

Little is known of the life of George Simeon Mwase. His typescript betrays few personal details, and his descendants can say little about his early life. Since the Government of Nyasaland employed him for the first time as a postal clerk in 1905, and since Africans customarily commenced their education in late adolescence, we may surmise that he was born into the Tonga tribe about twenty-five years before, i.e., about 1880. Mwase was the youngest of the three sons of Kapekenya, the hereditary younger brother of Chief Ngombo of Chipayika, near Chinteche in the modern Nkhata Bay district of northern Nyasaland. His eldest brother, Yesaya Zerenji Mwasi (who spelled his surname in a manner equally acceptable linguistically), was a prominent church and religious separatist leader who founded both the "Blackman's Church of God Which Is in Tongaland" and a number of African political associations. George Mwase received an education in the Bandawe school of the Free Church of Scotland. He may well have later attended the Overtoun Training Institution at Livingstonia, where he could have obtained skills sufficient to qualify as a postal worker.

In that capacity he was stationed at Chiromo, in the low, humid, riverine region of southern Nyasaland. Possibly he disliked the conditions there, for in the following year, 1906, he resigned and entered the administrative service of Northeastern (subsequently Northern) Rhodesia. Presumably as a postal clerk, although he may also have served in a regiment of the King's African Rifles, he remained in the employ of that government until 1920. Then he returned to Nyasaland, obtained a position as a tax clerk, and was stationed first at Lilongwe and, between 1922 and 1924, at Dedza. In that year he again resigned in order to trade on his own account in Lilongwe.

In 1927, while he still owned a store in Lilongwe, he became a politician. He organized the Central Province Universal Native Association (the acting provincial commissioner subsequently compelled Mwase to cease using the word "universal") in order "merely to bring to the notice of the Government all the grievances we now undertake through a misunderstanding of the Native feeling by Government." As the association's president and secretary, he presided over its first official meeting in a Lilongwe church. He suggested that Europeans would become aware of indigenous grievances only if Africans spoke with "a good voice." The membership of the association then urged the government to provide Africans with improved educational facilities. They demanded (probably at Mwase's instigation) that the government reduce the rental obligations of African storekeepers. "Why," a resolution asked, "the Government is so hard on native traders by asking them to pay rent on a store in his own country besides poll tax?" The association also deplored the treatment that African tenants received on white-run plantations and, in sentences that read like sections of Mwase's "Dialogue," complained that employers whipped their workers and provided them with food that was unfit to eat.[23]

The sixty members of the association apparently met twice a year, under the leadership of Mwase and James Ralph Nthinda Chinyama, who later became the president of the Nyasaland African Congress. The aim of the association, the members said, was "justice." [24] They continued to criticize conditions of African tenants, urged the government to establish produce markets, and objected strongly to the compulsory shifting of African villages which, they said, "is causing a lot of feelings of slavery." Since Mwase defended Asians in his "Dialogue," it is of interest that the association condemned them as the "swindlers and maltreaters of Africans." The minutes of a meeting in 1928 show that Mwase demanded "rights to use the products and the animals of the land." [25]

Although Mwase remained a politician, his venture into the commercial world ended in bankruptcy. In 1930, he became clerk to the district commissioner, Blantyre, and, without him and Chinyama, the Central Province Native Association became temporarily moribund. In March 1931, a local magistrate convicted Mwase of theft by a servant of the state; he embezzled taxes by manipulating the book of receipts.[26] Sentenced

23. NC 1/3/2: Minutes of a meeting of the Central Province Universal Native Association, 19 November 1927, Zomba archives.
24. NC 1/3/2: Unsigned memorandum of 27 January 1928.
25. NC 1/3/2: Minutes of meetings of 19 December 1927, 21 April 1928, and 30 March 1929.
26. NC 4/1/1: J. C. Abrahams to the Chief Secretary, 3 January 1933; Creasey to the editor, 10 August 1965. At the time of the embezzlement, Mwase was serving in a sub-boma near Mwanza in the Blantyre district.

to two years in prison, he apparently served only about sixteen months, and then retired to a village in the Lilongwe district.

During the late 1930's, Mwase again appears in the official records as a member and officer of native associations. He began at the same time to bombard the Chief Secretary and governor of the Protectorate with communications. Among them were many tracts in which he made a somewhat confusing case in favor of one of the several claimants to the paramount chieftaincy of the Tonga tribe. He also proposed different ways by which the tribe might be reorganized in keeping with the newly introduced Native Authority system. Occasionally he advanced his own claims of chiefly descent. Privately, some administrators thought that Mwase was a trifle dotty. As a result of his interference in a succession dispute in the Lilongwe district, administrators also deemed Mwase troublesome. The government therefore returned him to Chinteche, his original home in the West Nyasa district, and there placed him under restriction for about four years.

Mwase joined the Nyasaland African Congress shortly after its formation in 1944 and played a prominent role in its affairs. Initially, by virtue of his leading role in associational activity in Lilongwe, he sat on the executive committee of the Congress. In 1946, when Dr. H. Kamuzu Banda offered to pay the wages of an organizing secretary of the Congress, Mwase promised to provide an office. (The Congress refused both offers.) At that time, and for some years thereafter, he lived near the Diampwe River, midway between Lilongwe and Dedza. (Mwase apparently owned land and some stores in the district.) He strenuously opposed the successful British attempt to include Nyasaland within a white-dominated Central African Federation. Later, however, he became alienated from his fellow members of the Congress. A rebel to the end, he supported the Federation in the late 1950's, presented a memorandum to the Devlin Commission of Inquiry in which he decried the rapid pace of political change, and, despite his advanced years, stood forlornly (and forfeited his electoral deposit) as a United Federal Party candidate for Dedza in the 1961 elections that swept Dr. Banda's party into power. [27] His death on 3 August 1962 created little stir.

In 1965, people in the Bandawe area remembered Mwase as an exceptionally "clever" man who had managed to "trick" the colonial government and to perform various legendary feats of magic. He was credited with managing to make leaves look like money. It was also said that he had at various times married five wives and sired thirty-one children.

The editor has been unable to locate any mention of Mwase or his "Dialogue" in the published literature on Nyasaland. Neither missionaries nor administrators mention him, and his sojourn in Northern Rhodesia seems to have escaped the notice of all those whose writings have been preserved in print or in the files retained in the Lusaka archives.

27. Lord Devlin chaired the commission that investigated the emergency of 1959 in Nyasaland. See *Report of the Nyasaland Commission of Inquiry*, Cmnd. 814 (1959). The evidence submitted to the commission was not published.

A NOTE ON THE TEXT AND THE EDITING

The text that follows is copied from the only known extant example of what George Simeon Mwase originally entitled "A Dialogue of Nyasaland Record of Past Events, Environments & the Present Outlook within the Protectorate." This is an 86-page foolscap typescript that is held by the National Archives of Malawi as file NC 4/1/1. (A photostatic copy was used in the preparation of the present book.)

The typescript of Mwase's "Dialogue" may be the original. But Mwase wrote at least the first part of his commentary during 1931–32, when he was an inmate of the Zomba Central Prison. There he probably did not have access to a typewriter, and probably composed the "Dialogue" by hand. The typescript shows evidence of being copied: many spelling mistakes are inconsistent and blank spaces occur—one of them subsequently filled in by an unknown hand. If Mwase himself had copied his own handwritten account, there presumably would have been no blanks. There would probably have been consistency of error. The editor therefore surmises that Mwase's original version was begun by him during his stay in prison and probably completed in late 1932, after he had been released and was living under police supervision in a village in the Lilongwe district.

Mwase himself probably brought the "Dialogue"

to the attention of the Government of Nyasaland. The typescript in the file bears a covering note, dated 3 January 1933, from J. C. Abrahams, then Assistant Chief Secretary, to the Chief Secretary of the Protectorate, who on the same day sent it to Sir Hubert Young, the governor of Nyasaland. Abrahams indicated that he had obtained the "Dialogue" from S. S. Murray, an administrator who had compiled two editions of the fact-filled *A Handbook of Nyasaland* (London, 1922 and 1932). Murray thought that the governor might like to see the "Dialogue" in order "to enable him to form some estimate of the mental capabilities of the native." Sir Hubert minuted: "Interesting." The editor suspects that Mwase gave the typescript to Murray partially in order to secure himself official favor and, perhaps, attention.

Although the editor doubts that he has seen the original manuscript of Mwase's narrative and although the provenance of the typescript is uncertain, he has retained every word in the typescript—with the exception of cases of accidental dittography. (For example, "He He showed" has been silently changed to "He showed.") He has retained Mwase's word order, even though it is frequently unusual, and has changed no words with the aim of improving Mwase's grammar. The editor was tempted many times to depart from this rule, but there would be no clear end to this kind of tampering with what is, after all, the only text that we possess.

On the other hand, the editor has not hesitated to improve the readability of the text in minor ways where he could feel certain that the meaning would not be altered thereby. It would be pedantic to give such a haphazard typescript the verbatim treatment accorded to some precious medieval manuscript. The editor has thus silently made changes in:

(1) Spelling.

(2) Capitalization, where obvious slips of the typewriter have occurred, and where the typescript is inconsistent without apparent reason (for example, "Planter" and "planter," "Negro" and "negro," "Askari" and "askari").

(3) Other accidental inconsistencies of usage. For example, the typescript fluctuates at random among "whiteman," "white man," and "white-man." Because "whiteman" is by far the most frequent version, the other two have simply been treated as mistakes and silently corrected.

(4) Punctuation, where unorthodox practices, especially the indiscriminate use of commas, impede smooth reading. It was difficult to know precisely how to juggle commas and periods and to separate one sentence from another. When in doubt about the meaning, the editor has usually refrained from altering Mwase's punctuation.

(5) Paragraphing. Mwase did very little of it. Sometimes a whole chapter is given in one vast paragraph. The editor has divided such passages for easier reading.

Besides the invisible changes just described, the editor has attempted to make the narrative more meaningful by annotation and by the occasional use of two kinds of bracketed interpolations.

All footnotes are by the editor (Mwase supplied none).

Everything in brackets has been inserted by the editor. But everything in ordinary curved parentheses ( ) was Mwase's.

Single brackets [ ] are used to insert what appear to be missing words. This device is used only when the omission slows the reading appreciably. It is not used in hundreds of instances where the reader will automatically supply words (especially articles) as he goes along.

Angled brackets ⟨ ⟩ are used to "translate" or explain terms that might be obscure to many readers. For example, "B. I. Mission" is rendered "B. I. ⟨Baptist Industrial⟩ Mission." They are also used to clarify particularly obscure phrases in the text.

STRIKE A BLOW AND DIE ●

ORIGINAL TITLE: *A Dialogue of Nyasaland Record of Past Events, Environments & the Present Outlook within the Protectorate*

When at the first I took my pen in hand, that for
to write, I did not understand that I at all should make
any kind of a book in any kind of mode. Yea, I have un-
dertaken a risk of so-doing, have encouraged myself to
carry on with it, which, when almost done, made me to be
aware of its modification therein.[1]

I find not that I am denied the use of this my method,
so I do not mean to abuse when putting in the words and
comparison of things of old and new thereon, nor I mean
to [be] rude [in] the handling of any authority, power, nor
with the intent of harming one or all in my applica-
tion, but, all that I may seek the advantage of experience,
this or that way.

I know that there are men who are high as trees in wisdom and knowledge, who will write dialogue wise; yet,
none of them, in this country has done a slight of them
⟨done this in the slightest?⟩ yet. Indeed if I abuse the
power or authority[2] in my own composing of this, take
clearly that such abuses are due to inexperience, do not
grasp it wrongly and compare ⟨judge?⟩ it an impudent.
Anything wrongly recorded or wrongly compared I did
not mean to put in such unfavourable means at all. I
know and believe that my book will not be appreciable

1. The sense of "modification" is not clear.
2. A reference to the British colonial government of Nyasaland,
and to whites in general.

one in the eyes and feelings of the great men. Therefore anything wrongly written in is due to inadequate of knowledge and not to be taken as an insolent.

George S. Mwase.

● THE EDUCATION ON CHILEMBWE'S ACTIONS AND DEEDS: *A VERBIS AD VERBA* (FROM WORDS TO BLOWS)

I am conceived that the public will, I perceive, be instructed to read, and know much more of one, namely John Chilembwe of Chiradzulu, Nyasaland, of whom, anyone can bear witness of what suddenly happened him and the local Government, though it is seventeen years ago now.[1]

The purpose of writing this into a book, is because some people say that, and the other say this—so having met an eye witness who can, indeed, expound the whole story, and actions done true enough, I thought it the best to take every word from him in writing, and if possible form a book for the interest of the public and others who may be interested in the matter.[2]

Most of people know John Chilembwe only by name, which name, they have heard from other people talking and mentioning; but they do not know:

(1) Where John Chilembwe was born?
(2) What tribe John Chilembwe was?

1. Mwase apparently wrote in 1931–32; he refers here to the period of Chilembwe's militancy, i.e., 1914–15.
2. Mwase had many friends and contacts who might have played parts in the Chilembwe conspiracy. The "eye witness" mentioned was almost certainly Wallace Kampingo, a Chilembwe follower who was still in Zomba Central Prison when Mwase entered it in 1931. See the Introduction.

3

(3) Where John Chilembwe's progenitors came from?
(4) Where John Chilembwe received his Education?
(5) By [and] through whom John Chilembwe received Education?
(6) What year he came back from America?
(7) What year he opened his Mission at Chiradzulu?
(8) What was his behaviour and how people regarded him, with regard his teaching and soforth?
(9) What provoked him to form a rebellion against his Government?
(10) What orders he gave to his men before they fell into a conflict?[3]

It will be also, I am sure, interest to other people to know how that trouble was arranged out by the Rebels, as they are so-called; and how far they went with it either rightly or wrongly.

As the Protectorate is now developing, it has struck my mind that such events [which] happened sometime back should be recorded for the interest of the

---

3. When Mwase wrote the present book, answers to most of these questions were known to historians only circumstantially. To whites, at least, Chilembwe had already become a mythological figure. Only a few of Mwase's ten points were touched upon in the official report of the Chilembwe rising, *Report of the Commission Appointed by His Excellency the Governor to Inquire into Various Matters and Questions Concerned with the Native Rising within the Nyasaland Protectorate*, 6819 (Zomba, 1916). Similarly, Norman Leys, *Kenya* (London, 1924), 325–334, wrote of Chilembwe in general terms, and L. S. Norman, in "Rebellion," *Blackwood's Magazine*, CCXXX (1931), 862–873, presented only a partial picture of the events of the rising of 1915. In 1958, while Mwase's account still lay unknown in the Nyasaland archives, George Shepperson and Thomas Price supplied answers to many questions about Chilembwe in their *Independent African: John Chilembwe and the Origins, Setting and Significance of the Nyasaland Native Rising of 1915* (Edinburgh). In his own explication of the ten questions, Mwase adds important new information and amplifies some of the material contained in *Independent African*.

future generation of both White and African races to read and know of it, rather than they to hear wrongly explained to them of what occurred before them by their great grandfathers.[4]

This is, I believe, the civilised way to keep incidents being recorded in writing [rather] than in brains. My mind, therefore, has forced me to follow Chilembwe's back and onward up to his last contest, or up to his [last] being seen alive. I cannot, of course, know what happened to him after his death. I mean after he was shot and killed in the struggle.[5]

I am afraid, that some of the wise people will, I presume, be not interested when reading this poor book of mine, they will dislike the forming of such, and also will, I suppose, hate the name of the book,[6] and probably abhor the sound of its words therein. Yea, they will also dislike the very name of a person who has, indeed, composed such, even to wish bad luck on him, and all around him.

I therefore appeal to all such people to speak and hearken it diligently as one hearkens to a tiny bird singing in the wilderness, in which song he does not

4. A fellow Tonga who was politically active in South Africa had already expressed similar sentiments to a correspondent in Nyasaland: "Yes, I [have] heard [about] that African patriot John Chilembwe and I am indeed proud of his name. It was a few days ago that I was relating his adventure to my staff at this office and they were indeed inspired. Further particulars about him will be very much appreciated as I would like to obtain more information for [the] future history of Africa as I believe that the white men will not preserve the genuine history of the black man." S 2/28/21: Clements Kadalie to Isa Macdonald Lawrence, 4 April 1925, Zomba archives.

5. See below, 52. See also Robert I. Rotberg, *The Rise of Nationalism in Central Africa: The Making of Malawi and Zambia 1873–1964* (Cambridge, Mass.: Harvard University Press, 1965), 91.

6. It will be recalled that the title of Mwase's manuscript was "A Dialogue of Nyasaland Record of Past Events, Environments & the Present Outlook within the Protectorate."

pick, nor understand one word; but he pays attention only to the sound of its voice, and not the words. I know that, out of a hundred per cent, only ten per cent will understand the exposition of this book while ninety per cent will stand obstinate. Yea, some will call me a fool, and some will call me a crazed-headed coxcomb, even though a Legion.[7] But I call for your meditation upon the matter; you might, perhaps, after all, come to the conclusion of my idea, in recording the last misconception which misled people to form a struggle.[8]

I am very sorry to express my deep regret to have recorded such in English, by which language, I am not origin, even not a good speaker of the language, but as the language is ?Lingua Fraula? ⟨*lingua franca*⟩ in the Protectorate, I therefore venture to write my book in English. I call therefore for your assistance, you the speakers of the better tongue of the English language, to correct the errors, and to fill in the proper word instead, because I meant it. Certainly, the word which is wrongly recorded in [my book] I did not mean it, so the word correctly put in, I meant so.[9]

I reckon it hard enough to gather up the brains and minds of thousands, to come to agree to an idea

7. Mwase probably alludes to Mark 5:8–9: "For he said unto him, Come out of the man, thou unclean spirit. And he asked him, What is thy name? And he answered, saying, My name is Legion: for we are many."

8. It is not clear to what "misconception" Mwase refers.

9. Although English had been the language of governmental business for many years, Mwase himself would probably have had no more than four years of formal schooling in English. In church schools he would have learned to read Biblical passages in English as well as in Cinyanja and Citumbuka; in government employ he would have learned to write official letters. He would, however, have possessed little experience in expository writing. And the present book may represent a first draft.

formed by one brain, especially by a brain of a low class person such as myself. I mean in education and civilisation.

In view of certain circumstances to arise, in regard the framing of this book, [10] I earnestly beg a franchisement of mine mistakes, which has been due to dark of my perception that such will be, perhaps, apologised ⟨excused⟩. This is clearly known to all honourable people and others, that to form a book is quite easy enough, but to collect words for the book is very heavy than the weight of a living elephant. Yea, it is stiff, even expensive in time. Evidently, one can heap up a very long oration, but he is not a good orator, yet has heaped the speech for the good orators. I am one of the former, who is only stepping into, while the latters will be good authors.

We have, already, lost a considerable amount of our old histories etc. which, I am sure, would be of more interest to the present and future generations of both the African themselves and the Europeans as well.[11] If every events and incidents were then recorded in writing, there would be, I presume, not much argument with regard the paramount chief in the Protectorate, and so on.[12] This would also cost less time and money by the Government to follow things correctly,

10. Mwase began this book in prison, as he makes clear later.
11. The author refers both to the traditional, orally recounted, histories of whole peoples and clans and to the African view of the events in which Europeans played a part, and which until very recently were recounted solely by white writers, most of whom failed to use African evidence.
12. Mwase alludes to the numerous controversies over the legitimacy of those chiefs appointed by the Government of Nyasaland. He wrote during a period when the administrators of the Protectorate were attempting to introduce indirect rule. Mwase himself expended a great deal of energy upon the question of which chiefs should be accorded seniority among the Tonga.

than it is now, as they are (the Government) taking much trouble to find out what, and how such was carried out or done. This unintentional[13] error was due [to:] (1) No alphabet letters were known by our ancestors, although Islamic alphabets were in vicinity: and they thought to become an Islam was terrible; and they were afraid that, to know the Islam alphabet letters would also mean to make them to become people of that religion, which, I proceed ⟨suppose?⟩, that they were afraid that the religion was rigid, principally the use of dead-already game etc.[14] (2) They had not a slightest idea, that the country will change from the worse to better development. (3) They had no dream or suggestion that there will come another race of people such as Europeans to develop the country.

13. By the use of "unintentional," Mwase presumably attempts to prevent British officials from taking offense.

14. Swahili-speaking Arab and African traders from eastern Africa probably had commercial intercourse with the peoples of Malawi—the Nyasaland of Mwase's day—from about the fourteenth century. Before about the seventeenth century, these traders probably possessed an imperfect knowledge of the Qur'an; in their time, the ability to write Arabic may have been confined to the ruling class. But, from about the late seventeenth century, the Yao peoples of the Lake Malawi basin began to play a part in the slave trade. Many became Muslims; some therefore learned to communicate in the Arabic script, although in this script they probably wrote Swahili, not Arabic.

It is not completely clear why Mwase thought that his forefathers feared the conversion to Islam. The people of Malawi believed generally in an otiose diety. Ancestors provided a channel of communication thereto, and the Malawi peoples naturally propitiated their ancestors in ways that may have appeared to transgress the teachings of the Qur'an. Mwase, educationally the product of a Christian mission school, cannot be regarded, however, as an authority on reasons for, or even the fact of, his forefathers' resistance to the teachings and spread of Islam. "Dead-already game" refers to the Muslim requirement (derived from the Mosaic law) that meat destined for human consumption must derive from animals that have had their throats cut before death, preferably by an Imam. To Nyasas, who never had abundant supplies of meat, it seemed absurd to refuse to eat meat because the animal had not been killed in a manner prescribed by ritual.

8

So I see that our ancestors have deserted their narrative of their life time. Therefore, we should not be fool again to neglect our own, in our life time, for the benefit of our future offspring.

Following the truth, that all other colonies, I may say most of them, have recorded their long past incidents, and they still keep recording for the fresh happenings, my mind has instructed me impressively, to begin to open the way of framing something, such as books and the like, so to set an example for the grandchildren to do their best in them.

It is apparently true, that since the whiteman has opened the Protectorate[15] no book as yet has been put forward by the natives themselves for the benefit of their children.[16] I do not mean that there has

15. Between 1880 and 1890.
16. However, Yohanna B. Abdallah, an Anglican clergyman, had already written *Chiikala Cha Wayao*. It had been translated by Meredith Sanderson as *The Yaos*, and published in 1919 in Zomba by the Nyasaland Government Printer. Earlier, a manuscript by Andrew Nkonjera of Livingstonia mission was forwarded by A. D. Easterbrook, a district commissioner then resident in Lilongwe, to the Royal African Society of Great Britain. The Society published Nkonjera's "History of the Kamanga Tribe of Lake Nyasa" in the *Journal of the African Society*, X (1911), 331–341; XI (1912), 231–234. Saulos Nyirenda of Karonga, a telegraphist who worked for the African Trans-Continental Telegraph Company and who had once studied at the Livingstonia mission, had even earlier written on a similar subject. Although composed in 1908 or 1909, his "History of the Tumbuka-Henga People," translated by the missionary T. Cullen Young, did not appear until 1931 (*Bantu Studies*, V, 1–75). In Young's *Notes on the History of the Tumbuka-Kamanga Peoples in the Northern Province of Nyasaland* (London, 1932), which was a revised edition of a part of his *Notes on the Speech and History of the Tumbuka-Henga Peoples* (Livingstonia, 1923), he included four sections written by Africans. Amon Mwakasungula, Mark Mwakawanga, and Patrick Mwamlima wrote chapter vii (62–78), "The Ngonde Point of View"; and Yuraya C. Chirwa, "Relationship between the Tonga and the Ngoni," wrote chapter xiii (127–130). The other two contributions were anonymous. Levi Mumba's "The Religion of My Father," in *The International Review of Missions*, XIX (1930), 362–376, had already appeared. Even earlier the Rev. Mr. Donald Fraser had

been not one man who could be able to write words for the purpose of making a book. Nay, indeed, millions of them can do so, but the only reason is that such thoughts have not struck them. It is always the case everywhere, around the wide world, that useful methods of making, or doing something good, bad or popular, are to brought into the notice of many, by one particular person, and that, indeed, will remind the wise people to think deep or if possible beyond the first person's methods. As for instance, the methods of one Sir (was he knighted before or after?) Isaac Newton, with regard the boiling kettle by which he adopted the methods of making a steamer, of course, he made one for a trial, although coarse. Then other wise people thought more deeply and tried their best to form [steamers] in this way or the other. At last they were succeeded in building better steamers, these we now see; so [it] does not matter who has built a better steamer, but he has built it in the methods formed by Sir Isaac and we call Sir Isaac the first and great Inventor of steamers.[17]

There has been a great change since then, and such changes must be recorded for the future generation to know what and when. There is indeed a greater change of outlook now than it was expected. Notwithstanding, so say that, the relationship between the

popularized and retold the autobiography of Daniel Mtusu, a Ngoni, in *The Autobiography of an African* (London, 1925). But, except for Abdallah's book, Mwase's contention remained valid until the publication of Samuel Yosia Ntara (trans. and ed. T. Cullen Young), *Man of Africa* (London, 1934), and Yesaya Mlonyeni Chibambo (trans. Charles Stuart), *My Ngoni of Nyasaland* (London, 1942).

17. Mwase apparently confused Newton with James Watt. The condensing steam-engine emerged in 1789 when Watt perfected the engine of Thomas Newcomen; this in turn made possible the steamers to which Mwase alludes.

races is now becoming closily enough ⟨closer?⟩, although certain of both people still look timorous.[18]

Before this change came on, there has been a great misunderstandings to both people, especially in the material ⟨material sphere?⟩, and even socially. White people did not like to pay attention to what black people had to say, does not matter important or not, and the latter race feared the former, and compared them as White Hobgoblins from Heaven, even apparitions of under water, while the former also compared the latter as an ape's descendants, yea, even Chimpanzee's family—all this turned the fundamental into vague, even into a staggering state.

Now let me go and find out where John Chilembwe was born, and what tribe he belonged, and after that, I will go on with the rest about him, and such other subjects [as] may arise.

18. Mwase goes on to write critically of the state of race relations in Malawi. This paragraph may therefore have been intended to disarm hostile white critics. Should "so say that" be "some say that"?

● CHILEMBWE'S PLACE OF BIRTH
& HIS PROPER TRIBE

As I have written already about finding the place where John Chilembwe was born. His birth place is Tsangano hill in the vicinity of Chiradzulu hill and district in the Protectorate. Most of our people know this place Tsangano.[1] He was born by a man, called Chilembwe by name, of the Yao, Phiri tribe, by his wife Nyangu, a woman of the Chewa tribe.[2]

[Nyangu was] originally great granddaughter of the family of Royal blood, of a great chief called *Kalonga Mphiri*, whose power of control was over all the [Nyasaland] Protectorate, [and over] Northern Rhodesia, half portion of Southern Rhodesia, even half or less of Portuguese East Africa in the southern portion, and so in the east as well [as] up to southern portion of Tanganyika Territory.[3] This great man, Kalonga, is

1. "Tsangano," in the modern orthography Sanganu, is located a few miles northeast of the Providence Industrial Mission at Mbombwe.
2. That is, John Chilembwe's father was a Yao, of the common Phiri (or "hill") clan. Chilembwe (antelope) was a personal name, not a family name in the Western sense. Marriage between Chewa (in modern orthography Cewa) and Yao was commonplace since the two tribal groups had, at least during the nineteenth century, intermingled throughout southern Malawi. With regard to Chilembwe's birthplace and tribal background, see below, 19. The account in George Shepperson and Thomas Price, *Independent African* (Edinburgh, 1958), 42–46, agrees substantially.
3. Kalonga or Karonga was the putative first king of the Malawi nation or confederation in about the seventeenth century. He is said, probably during the period when the Lunda/Luba empire

12

known by all the tribes in the Protectorate including
the places I have mentioned above. This great man,
at the arrival of all the tribes from far north, was
with them, but at that time, he was not greater than
the others, and he did not bear that name of Kalonga
even, he succeeded the greatness through leading others to explore some lands.[4] He was a cunning fox,
and very clever in his dealings, by that he won the
greatness above his tribesmen and all, yet, he was
called differently, and not Kalonga.

I will roughly explain, how he became to be called
Kalonga. I am very sorry to explain that as it stands
very far of my reach, but, I am able to explain it in
the way it was recorded in the heads of our old
fathers and others who also, I understand, received
such informations from their fathers and their fathers
from their great grandfathers.

Now I want to expound slightly how this great man
owned this name of Kalonga only, and not his second
⟨clan⟩ name "Mphiri," I will explain his second name
separately. As I have already said, that this man was
so great above others, and all. He then begun to wage
wars against other people and defeat them. And after
he had killed a lot of people lying dead in the field,
he then begun to cut the heads of the dead people and
pack them in baskets, bringing them to his village.
So he kept doing that all his time when even he has
killed some people either at the war or at any other

of Mwata Yamvo was undergoing internal strains, to have led the
Malawi people from what is now the Congo across modern Zambia
into modern Malawi, where his followers settled and later fractured
into a number of tribal groups, of which the Cewa today remain
pre-eminent.

4. In this sentence Mwase may have meant to say that Kalonga
"did not bear that name of Kalonga, even though he surpassed
them in greatness through leading others to explore."

time. When the people saw this often being done by him the people then called him *Kalonga*. That bears the meaning of packing. They meant to say that his name was *Packer*. One who packs heads of people into baskets. In this way, he owned the name of "Kalonga." [5]

Now following his second name *"Mphiri."* This explains as under written. When these [Malawi] people came from the far north, probably from the Ugogo, near Mombasa, they were led by an Arab.[6] That, I may say, it was some centuries ago. I may suggest that may be about 300 to 350 years ago. Less or more I am not sure, of course about the time. They arrived first at Henga, near Ekwendeni in the Mombera District.[7] (This was named Mombera District afterwards.)[8] There they camped near the hill called Choma in the same district. At that place their leader, the Arab, died, and they were left, by themselves; Kalonga then, moved his village from the level place, and built it on the top of that hill called Choma, leaving the rest on the plain. Immediately then, the people who were still on the plain place, called Kalonga and all his people with him, on the hill, to be Aphiri. That ob-

5. This account of the name of Karonga agrees with no other. But see T. Cullen Young, *Notes on the History of the Tumbuka-Kamanga Peoples in the Northern Province of Nyasaland* (London, 1932), 90.

6. This is an idiosyncratic version of Malawi history that finds no support in the literature. Ugogo is only relatively "near" Mombasa, being located in central Tanzania.

7. This conclusion finds no corroboration in T. Cullen Young, *Notes on the Speech and History of the Tumbuka-Henga Peoples* (Livingstonia, 1923), nor in any of the other standard discussions of the origins of the Malawi nation. The present name for Mombera is Mzimba.

8. The reader is reminded that ordinary parentheses are Mwase's. All interpolations by the editor are in [ ] and ⟨ ⟩.

viously means, that people who dwell or live on the top of a hill. Phiri means, Hill or mountain, either or both bear the same name Phiri. Kalonga and his people then called the people who were still on the plain, to be, Abanda. That means level or plain.[9] There from one tribe they begun to be two different tribes.

I do not like to go on beyond the limit of my memory, I mean with regard the tribes how they burst out, from one to two, and then to hundreds as they are now. Someone will, I am sure, go on with it sooner or later. Further, I say that before these people came from Ugogo Mombasa, this country was occupied by the dwarf people—so called Abatwa who were then driven away by the Wankhoma. Abatwa are now in the Congo Belge, still called Abatwa. Wankhoma was another tribe which occupied the whole of the Protectorate, from the Abatwa. Afterwards, these Wankhoma were defeated by great man, Kalonga, and were all annihilated and subdued. No big chiefs of these Wankhoma were then left to rule, up to this time in the Protectorate and the near vicinity.[10]

This explain, that John was not a man from another country, but that he belonged to this country. As I have already said, John was "Mphiri," a descendant of Kalonga the great, [but] I cannot explain, and nobody else will tell whether he was really of Kalonga's own family or out of the descendants of Kalonga's

9. The word "Banda" usually connotes an enclosure.
10. In many parts of tropical Africa the present occupants claim to have ousted an Abatwa or pigmy people. The name Twa has been used in eastern and central Africa to denote a smaller, autochthonous people whose language and physical traits differ markedly from the later Bantu-speaking invaders. In Mwase's day, the smaller people of Northern Rhodesia as well as the Belgian Congo and Ruanda-Urundi were known as Twa. See also W. H. J. Rangeley, "The Earliest Inhabitants," *The Nyasaland Journal,* XVI, 2 (1963), 36–40.

people who went to live with him on the top of a hill, for they were all called Aphiri, inclusively.[11]

These people when they left Ugogo, I suppose they were not expanded into many. Besides that, they had no "Pfuko," or "Mfunda," they were like Europeans who have no "Pfuko" or "Mfunda," but only the Sur-name, the family name of their grandfathers and so forth.[12] This tells out that when these people were coming from the north they were of one tribe, but who will tell what tribe they were? They may be Wagogo or the like—none can tell. I have gone far beyond the limit of my experience in touching the old history of our centuries past grandfathers and so forth.

I wish to touch John severely of his tribe first. Many people mistaken[ly think] that he was an Chipeta and others say an Anguru. I say he was neither of both, nay, he was never an Chipeta nor an Anguru, even any other tribe.[13] Who was he? He was a "Phiri," born out by the people who dwelt on the Choma Hill with Kalonga or by Kalonga's own family, nobody can tell. I say he was not an Chipeta; why? I will certainly tell, why he is not an Chipeta. The Chipeta does not apply to any people, but it applies to country, land of Chipeta; [which] means land of long and thick grass.[14] Therefore, no person can belong to the family

11. Joseph Booth, among others, never refers to Chilembwe as a descendant of Karonga (Kalonga). See also Shepperson and Price, *Independent African*, 44.

12. *Pfuko* or *fuko* is Cinyanja for "clan" or "tribe." *Mfunda* expresses kinship or a blood relationship.

13. The author, like other Nyasas, apparently viewed the Nguru people, originally of Moçambique but latterly of Nyasaland, with contempt.

14. Although Mwase gives its correct literal meaning, there were Nyasas and Moçambiquans who nevertheless gave their tribal name as Chipeta. The Chipeta are generally considered Cewa.

of long grass, or thick grass, whatever it may be called. The people in that thick or long grass country are the "Aphiri" and the "Abanda" respectively. They are the offspring of the Aphiri and the Abanda generally —the two are cousins at the first place. So to call John an Anguru is totally wrong.

He was born by a woman called "Nyangu." This name, "Nyangu," applies to high birth of either the "Aphiri" descendants or the Abanda. [Whether] this name Nyangu has come from Ugogo or further I cannot say. What I can describe about this very name, is that the whole tribes in the Protectorate and all the adjourned ⟨adjoining⟩ countries have kept this name given to one, who supposed to have been born out of high family.[15] By this time, of course, any other people may have opportunity of taking it for themselves. As it has been done to the name of a great man, Kalonga, now anyone uses it at any time he likes, for he knows there will be no queries from anyone or anywhere. This woman Nyangu is a "Mphiri" of the descendant of Kalonga the great or out of the Kalonga's people [who] dwelt on the hill Choma. This name Nyangu applies also to mother of Chief Undi, who is the nephew to Kalonga the great [and] who was also given a full control by his uncle Kalonga of the whole northern portion of all the Portuguese East Africa and the eastern portion of Northern Rhodesia as well.[16]

This clears out the doubts that John was not of any other tribe, but that he was born out of a woman who indeed had some connection which ⟨with⟩ the

15. Mwase is alone in suggesting that the name derives from Ugogo. Usually it is attributed to an ancestress of the Malawi nation.

16. During Mwase's day, Undi's successor resided in Northern Rhodesia, where he was styled Paramount Chief of the Cewa.

family of that great man, either of his (the great man's) own family or by great man's people I cannot exactly say, and no one else will.

As I said above, that his father was also a "Mphiri" whom later on was tribed to Yao. There is no tribe Yao, as far as I can recollect, but I find, there is a hill called Yao, in the Portuguese East Africa near the boundary of Portuguese East Africa and the late German East Africa now Tanganyika Territory. I do not like to go on so deep about his father origin. I roughly say, he was a Mphiri, who, from the information obtained broke out from the great man and astrayed over that country which lies near the hill called Yao. It is there then they owned the tribe of Yao as you see it exist up to this time.[17] Secondly, I do not like to go further with John's father, for he was not an inheritor of the father, but mother, for that is the custom ruling in the Protectorate and many other countries in the adjoining vicinity, with the exception of the Angoni (Zulu) who broke out from the tyrant Chaka and his successor Dingani, [and who] are the only tribe in the Protectorate whose inheritance is from their fathers, although other tribes are gradually adopting it, but not so very many of them do so. I might say, it is the best scheme than the other.

John after being born at Tsangano came to live at the Michiru in the Blantyre District (formerly called Kukabula) with his mother and father as well. This

17. Most Yao would dispute Mwase's conclusions with regard to their existence. The Yao traditionally say that they came from the hill noted by Mwase. See W. H. J. Rangeley, "The Ayao," *Nyasaland Journal*, XVI, 1 (1963), 7–27; Thomas Price, "Yao Origins," *ibid.*, XVII, 2 (1964), 11–16. See also J. Clyde Mitchell, *The Yao Village: A Study in the Social Structure of a Nyasaland Tribe* (Manchester, 1956), 22.

woman Nyangu was previously married to another man while she was still at Msinja or somewhere in the Dedza District or at Mawereanyangu in the Ncheu District. This husband had three children by her, one of her three children is Mpinganjila, a chief or a Government Councillor, in the Fort Johnston District. His village lies southward of Fort Johnston Boma, it is near the Boma itself.[18] The present Mpinganjila is the nephew of the predecessor, who was a real son of this woman Nyangu. The mother of John—Chief Mpinganjila of Fort Johnston was her second son, after Chimpere, who was her first son by the first husband; the first husband's name I cannot possibly mention now. He died after giving her three children. Two sons Chimpere and Mpinganjila and one daughter. After first husband had died, Chilembwe married her and had two children by her, John and his sister; altogether she had five children.

Nyangu first lived with [the] late [senior chief] Kuntaja after she left Tsangano hill, together with her second husband and children, at a place where Blantyre Boma is built. Kuntaja was asked to move that site by the Government for the purpose of building [a] Boma, there, so he moved to Michiru. Nyangu and her husband with children all removed together with Kuntaja to Michiru.

I trust I have explained far enough about John's place of birth, and of what tribe he was, even where he originally came from and all his ancestors and the like. In the position of all the evidence and informations obtained, I am apt to expose the whole story and nothing will be kept enigma.

18. *Boma* = an administrative headquarters. A place called Masinja is located due north of Dedza.

● WHERE JOHN'S EDUCATION WAS RECEIVED?

Now I am replying [to] the question about John's education. John at the first place was a scholar of the Church of Scotland Mission School, Blantyre.[1] There he gained the knowledge of reading and writing as well, and was also a member of that Church as a Catechumen, but was not baptised then. Later on, it was heard that at Mandala[2] outside their premises, has camped another whiteman from Europe with the intention of opening other Schools and Churches. John then went there to see if that was true. There he saw one adult European with his young girl. The whiteman told him that he was Joseph Booth, from Europe, with the intention of opening Schools and Churches in the country.[3] He told John that on his way coming was accompanied by his wife and the child, and that, his wife had died on the way some-where, and that he has reached with the young girl only. Mr. Joseph Booth then, asked John if he could take work [as] a nurse to his daughter. This job, John

1. About 1890. Shepperson and Price, in *Independent African,* 442, tend to agree.
2. Mandala, near Blantyre, was the headquarters of the African Lakes Corporation.
3. Booth was a Baptist missionary. Hitherto, the only Western schools in the southern part of the Protectorate had been sup-ported by the Church of Scotland.

agreed [to] at the same time, and started it straight-
way.[4]

While he was doing this work, as a nurse, was also
working as a house boy, and all the time he attended
the Church sermonies ⟨ceremonies? sermons?⟩ of Mr.
Booth, and afterwards was baptised by him. This
time, there came to Mr. Booth one Golden Mataka,
who was also baptised and was also one of Mr.
Booth's men.[5] After that he gathered a lot of people.
Some time after, Mr. Booth put John on teaching
work and [John] was a teacher and a preacher as
well. When Mr. Booth was forming the Zambezi Industrial Mission, N. I. ⟨Nyasa Industrial⟩ Mission, B. I.
⟨Baptist Industrial⟩ Mission, and the Seventh day
Adventist [mission] which is now known as "Malamulo" Mission, John was with Mr. Booth. Later, I
cannot say how many years after, he was a teacher
at Mitsidi. Mr. Booth sent John to take charge of
a river boat in the Chikwawa District which was carrying loads from Chindio ⟨Chinde⟩ to Thema for Mr.
Booth.[6]

John carried this work for some time probably, for
some years, I cannot tell how many, till Mr. Booth
was compelled to leave the Protectorate, under what
circumstances I cannot explain.[7]

4. It seems likely that these events have been telescoped in
Mwase's narration.

5. Golden, or Gordon, Mathaka joined Booth at Mitsidi in 1893.
He later turned against him.

6. Booth encouraged the establishment of the Baptist Industrial
Mission of Scotland at Gowa, in Nyasaland, but did not "form"
it. The Seventh-day Adventists purchased the Malamulo station
in 1901 after Booth had broken with the Seventh Day Baptists,
for whom he had originally opened it. With regard to the steamer,
see Shepperson and Price, *Independent African*, 59, 445.

7. Booth left voluntarily to go to Britain and the United States

Mr. Booth left the Protectorate, took the route towards where John was with the boat; and asked John to accompany him further. John then accompanied Mr. Booth, who took him on to America and handed him over to Rev. a Mr. [Lewis Garnett] Jordan of the Providence Industrial Mission in America. This is a pure Negroes Industrial Mission there, and it is controlled by pure Negroes of America. John was then put into the Negroes' College in America.[8] Mr. Booth left him there and returned back to South Africa. I cannot go on [with] what was done by Mr. Booth with regard to the education of John while in America. John after passing his theology courses was ordained to be a Minister of the Providence Industrial Mission.[9] I do not say how many years he remained in America before or after he was ordained to a Ministership. Pastor John (as he was then called) was asked to return back home into this Protectorate to open a branch of that Mission.[10]

He agreed to do so, and left America for Nyasaland. I cannot mention what month he left America for

---

with Chilembwe in 1897. He sought financial support and hoped to further Chilembwe's education. In 1899, as a result of governmental hostility, Booth fled the country and stayed away for several months. It is conceivable that Mwase confused the two occasions.

8. Lewis Garnett Jordan was the secretary of the National Baptist Convention, then the most powerful American Negro religious organization. Probably this is what Mwase meant when he wrote "Providence Industrial Mission," which is a name Chilembwe adopted for his African work. In America, Chilembwe attended the Virginia Theological Seminary and College at Lynchburg, Virginia, which was affiliated with the National Baptist Convention.

9. As far as the editor knows, the name has no specific American provenance. Presumably Chilembwe was ordained as a Baptist.

10. It is not clear by whom Chilembwe was asked to return. We have heretofore assumed that he returned home on his own initiative. Had Mwase read Booth's *Africa for the African* (Baltimore, 1897)?

Nyasaland. He arrived at Chinde some time in May or June 1899.[11] He wired to the Protectorate Government of his arrival there, and his intention of coming back, into the Protectorate for the purpose of opening a Mission. The reply was sent to him to wait a while, until further information could be obtained. John was then detained there until July of the same year, when he was allowed to come into the Protectorate. He arrived at Blantyre July 1899. He stayed with his mother till September of the same year.

Some time in September 1899 John left Blantyre, Michiru, to look a place for starting his Mission. He went to Chiradzulu and found a site, where the Mission was then erected. This place he owned ⟨bought⟩ it from the Government on behalf of the Mission. It was then published ⟨gazetted⟩ as Mission Freehold Land. I cannot state, how much he paid for the land to the Government.

John begun his Mission work in September 1900. He then progressed extremely. He had a great number of attendants etc. Afterwards, some time in 1901 Rev. L. N. Check ⟨Landon N. Cheek⟩ arrived from America for the purpose of aiding John at Chiradzulu. This Pastor was sent by the head of Providence Industrial Mission in America. He was a Coloured Negro. I do not know whether he was a Mulatto.[12] This man, Pastor Check, afterwards, married Rachel, the daughter of Chimpere, a uterine [brother] of John,

---

11. But 1900 is a more likely date. See Shepperson and Price, *Independent African*, 127, 454.

12. "Coloured" in Southern Africa meant and means mulatto. Mwase seems to distinguish between light and dark-skinned Negroes. He also wonders whether Cheek's (Mwase or his copyist consistently misspells it as Check) lightness of color stemmed from a mixed parentage.

and the first born son of Nyangu. In 1902 a Miss E[mma B.] DeLany was also sent from America to take up works as a Schoolmasteress. She was a pure Negro lady, of America.[13] She was unmarried.

The place then developed [faster] than it was expected at the first. There were at last a great number of School and Church members. In 1905 Miss DeLany left Chiradzulu some time in May [and] went back to America for good. Mr. Daniel S. Malekebu went after her the same year and month. Mr. Daniel (then Pastor Daniel) was working to Miss DeLany as a house boy before she went back to America.[14] At the same time he was also attending the School as well. In 1907 Pastor Check also left Chiradzulu for America. He took with him, his wife, Rachel, the daughter of Chimpere, [and] two sons of one Mr. Duncan Njilima (now dead) accompanied him to America. They were Mathew Njilima and Mr. Fred Gresham Njilima. The latter is now back into Protectorate leaving the former still in America up to this time.[15]

John was again left alone in charge of the *Chiradzulu Branch of the Providence Industrial Mission.*

13. In Mwase's typescript the name DeLany is spelled Deloyn here and Delayn hereafter. Mwase implies that Miss DeLany was darker and therefore "purer."

14. Apparently "then Pastor Daniel" ought to be "later Pastor Daniel." His full name was Daniel Sharpe Malekebu. The name was spelled "Malikebu" in Mwase's typescript.

15. In the typescript Mathew is spelled with two t's and Gresham is spelled "Grasham." Fred Gresham Njilima studied at a high school in Natchez, Mississippi, and attended colleges in Kentucky. The father, Duncan, was hanged as an accomplice of Chilembwe. See Rotberg, *Rise of Nationalism*, 119n.

● JOHN'S CHARACTER AND DEMEANOUR

John was a very good player of Limba (Harp),[1] that was before he became a good scholar of the Scotch Mission, but was very popular man all round. His deportment when a Missionary at Chiradzulu was excellent. He was very kind to every man, woman old and young. He always visited the sick in their death beds—does not matter [whether] a Christian of his Church or any other people around the villages near him and near vicinity. He mourned for the dead, and attended burials. He helped making Coffin for the dead if timbers were available and even to support ⟨supply?⟩ cloths for the dead person.[2] Old men and women he helped them by clothing them out of his own expense. He cared the sick by sending them on to Blantyre Mission Hospital on his Machilla and provided [them] with his own Macherero (Machillas carriers).[3]

He paid much attention to what one said or complained. He showed hospitality to strangers. Had no

1. The *kalimba* is a small autoharp, of varying size, the tines of which are vibrated manually. It is an instrument common to nearly all of tropical Africa.

2. Cloths? He may mean shrouds.

3. The *machila* is an African version of the sedan chair. It resembles a hammock slung beneath two poles that are carried by porters, and is a more sophisticated version of the stretcher. Europeans, fearing the tropical heat, often moved about the Protectorate in *machila*.

idea of sending away uneducated people and those poor in dressing before him. His benevolence was for all and not for choosing or cull ⟨culling?⟩ among the people. He loved to listen to youth as well [as] to an old person and to a Christian, as well [as] to a pagan. He was weak to arise angry ⟨slow to anger?⟩ but very rigid. He was a man who waited to see that the orders given out, must be carried out, and also must be carried in the same way he had issued it. Otherwise he became very much worried, [and would] probably chide the person who was referred into it, at his private office.

Besides that, John was a very hard worker. [Once] work commenced, he wanted to see it done. He was not only a good supervisor, but to do the work with his own hand also—people were well paid to their satisfactory. He collected the Church funds in the usual way, and [they] were deposited to the appointed Church Treasurer for the use of Church requirements etc. Never talked ostentatiously to anybody, nor to ⟨nor did he⟩ deliver a vaunting speech to the audience. He was not in habit of losing temper but on a special reason of course, he would look like it.

I do not like to record anything regard his private character and behaviour towards his family. I am recording only what interested the public view of the views. John was not a very healthy man, his built was clime ⟨slim? slight?⟩, one eye was out of proper sight. It was some time operated [on] by the Mission Doctor of Scotch Mission.[4] His colour was jet. He was fond of wearing a black suit; and on other occasions white and the like. He looked nice and clean. His habit was to invite friends to his table for food;

4. Probably Dr. Robert Macfarlane.

he was also a very good jester to his comrades, even a socialist of both racial and social ⟨he was sociable with both races?⟩.

His courtesy towards his country people was too ⟨very?⟩ great. He wished to see them educated and civilised or run for such, if possible. He never despised any other Schools or Churches in his personal doctrine. His aim was to direct his country people to go to any School for education, for that was the elementary to civilisation. He was highly respected by the people not [for] being a Missionary but for his examples towards them and all around him.

John was a good hunter of game. Whenever game [was] killed [it was] distributed to people free. He never missed his shot, but in certain occasions he could.

He was always sober, he hated any kind of drink and abhorred the power of alcohol. He exhorted people from keeping themselves into strong drinks, and such like, he taught adults and children to keep on work, not to lounge about, even to advise ⟨he even advised⟩ headmen [and] eldermen to keep their villages nice and clean telling them that was the key to civilisation, also the key to a good healthy [life], he often said, he liked to see his country men work hard and prosper in their undertakings, also to see them smart, such as Negro fellows he had seen in America and other countries. He preached against carnalist, murderer, robber, a burglar and a thief. He warned his country men against the habit of begging, he explained that begging was very much disgraceful system on the face of the world. People [who] go out for begging do not look vogue ⟨in good repute?⟩.

He often said he was very much sorry to see woman

—does not matter [if] pregnant, old woman, and the like—tied up round their stomach with a rope or a string in a now ⟨knot⟩ by the native Askari; as that was the system done in those days by the Boma Askari to arrest women for not paying hut tax.[5] The native Askari or Police whatsoever they were called were doing this in a very tremendous way. The Askari being pure brutes, who did not realize the value of their own women in the country. Shook the villages and villagers terribly. So that they did not believe that the Boma did not tell these brute Askaris to worry people in the villages. John often spoke to the brutes that the way they do was terrible. But no attention was paid to that. These troubles molested John deeply and even some other times he could not take his food as usual through ⟨because of⟩ these grievances which were put on his country and country people.

5. For a discussion of the hut tax system, see the introduction to this volume and Rotberg, *Rise of Nationalism*, 39–47.

● THE REAL CAUSE FOR FORMING A REBELLION AND HOW THE ARMY WAS DIVIDED AND HOW THEY FOUGHT TO THE END

Now let me dig out the real cause for John's rebellion against his local Government, and what was his personal intention.

Before I say more, I must strongly say that John had no intention of rebelling against the Government itself, but as the Government is the head of anything and hold ⟨is held⟩ responsible for any cause or reason, therefore I say he revolted against the Government. His personal aim was to fight white Planters, Traders, and other white settlers within the country.

From his own talk to the people. He said, the white Planters, Traders and other white settlers of the country, who are employers of native labour, were not treating their labourers well. They were paying them much less pay, 3/- for adult, native, sometimes less, for 30 days' ticket.[1] They were beaten either with Chikoti (whip) by the employer, without referring the case into the Boma, and for no proper reason for beating them.[2] They were being dismissed from the work after finishing some tickets without [the em-

---

1. In Central Africa wages were paid monthly. Since laborers sometimes failed to report for work on succeeding days, thirty working days—whether or not in succession—were reckoned as a month. At the end of each shift or day, a worker's ticket was stamped. When he had collected thirty stamps, and not before— it might take a month or a year—he received his pay.
2. The *chikoti* was a whip usually fashioned of cured rhinoceros hide.

ployers'] paying them, and often pay them in kind instead of cash. If he asks why, he is to be beaten and was told "Choka" (go away) ⟨scram!⟩. The Land-owners returned out ⟨evicted⟩ natives as they liked. They were holding courts of their own. Flogging natives on their lands, does not matter for what reason. Sending natives into the Boma with a letter and write anything true or lie. There the Boma accepted anything written by a whiteman and punish the poor native without calling the whiteman for his evidence personally. A native was often times beaten by a whiteman if he did not take off his hat off his head some thousands yards away, even a mile away of a whiteman. A native often met Shouts of Chotsa Chipewa (Take off your hat) in every corner he could go.[3] A native was given heavy load to carry (say from 80 lbs. to 90 or more sometimes) for some distance and for very small pay. If was unable to lift it, was to be beaten. Many people died on this Tenga-tenga ⟨porterage⟩ work. Some were dying on the road, and some on arrival at their village. The natives were moved by Planters etc. on their villages, telling them that he, the Planter has bought the land from the Boma without first consulting them. The natives very much astonished and know not what to do or where to go and live comfortable.

Secondly, John was excited when his prayer houses were totally burnt up by a Planter after allowing them to be built at the first place, but he did not threaten them, he only sighed and said "See the evil doing of these white Planters etc., in the country." He said if he ⟨the planter⟩ did not like our prayer

3. For the celebrated "affair of the solar topee," see Rotberg, *Rise of Nationalism*, 120–121.

houses to be built on his land he would ⟨should⟩ have stopped that at the first request, rather than to allow them [to be] built up and then destroy them by setting fire on them afterwards and also without any cause or reason for burning them.[4] This grieved his heart, of course. Was he preparing weapons this time? No, nothing at all.

There was also another bad example, which white Planters and friends were doing, in buying fowls, goats and such like for themselves from natives, not to pay the price asked for it, but to give anything the Planter thought, also throwing it when giving it to the native. That was also vediculous ⟨ridiculous⟩.

Thirdly, John said that the Government was quite slack and was biased to white Planters and others. He explained the reasons as follows: White Planters sent in natives with letters for punishment. The letters were used as evidence against the natives and punishments were inflicted on them. How they believed on the words in letters only? And that if native would denied the words, and said, no, the whiteman is, indeed, lying in his letter, this made the Resident ⟨the British administrative official⟩ angry, and [he would] say the whiteman does not lie, why you say he is lying? There natives wondered, why a whiteman should not lie, is he not a descendant of Adam and Eve, from whom, every kind of evil has started from, including lying and many other sins thereto, why a whiteman should not? Also that natives flogged by a Planter, or any other whiteman, or chased away with-

4. William Jervis Livingstone, the manager of the A. Livingstone Bruce estate that adjoined Chilembwe's Providence Industrial Mission, apparently in a wanton manner destroyed chapels erected on the estate without warning the Chilembwists or offering to discuss the matter with them.

31

out pay, to come and lay their complaints at the
Boma, they were again sent away with a word that
a whiteman cannot beat or chase you away without
a good cause, and [the Resident] telling them that,
if I will call the whiteman and if he will come and
say that you did wrong, then you will be beaten
again or put to prison. Being in those days the Boma
was bias to a whiteman's talk, the natives then returning home empty and not knowing where to pay
⟨make⟩ their complaints, at last they had to lose their
hope, the "Chotsa Chipewa" system was in full force
in the towns and outside, the Boma did not then de-
fend the natives from being beaten for his own Chipewa.

Another grievance John complained of himself was
about less supervision on the native Askari. The Boma
knew that the Askari were pure barbarians and would
do brutality on villagers, yet allowed them to trouble
the villagers as much they could, and all the blame
John put it on the Government who took no action
against the brutes, who being savages doing wrong
was much [more] valued by them than to follow orders
of their masters.[5]

Another reason [that] grieved John, was, about the
men of his country who had died in the wars, of
different countries, such as Somaliland and other countries previously, of whom the Government did not
look on their relatives even to help their wives and
children, who had lost their people, who were their
helpers. Their old mothers and fathers were asked,
say ⟨nay?⟩, forced to pay the tax, although their sons,
who were giving them money for tax, were killed at

5. Mwase means that the government depended upon the *askari;*
it therefore let them run amok.

the war, which war was nothing to do with them. Many people were recruited [in] 1902 for Jubaland war, or another I do not know which.[6] Very few of the recruited men returned back while the bigger number of people only names were brought back.

These grievances did not, as yet, took John into a deep thought of rising in arms against [any]body. He remained quiet. As things were as I have stated, John did not threaten either the Planter nor the Government. At last there came some rumours that war has broke out between British and the Germans. This rumour was heard some times in August 1914. This news reached John, who, after hearing it, waited what will happen again to his country men in regard recruiting more Askari, for the fresh war, or else they will be left alone.

Sometime in September 1914, he heard that the Boma was again recruiting more men of the country for the fresh war. Evidently he saw people being recruited for the war.[7] He then thought to write a letter which to be inserted in the paper, for the public to read. This letter was written in English, and [he] sent it to the Editor, of Nyasaland Times, Blantyre, with a request of publishing it for the public. The letter was written like this:

Dear friends, As I hear that, war has broke out between you and other nations, only whitemen, I request, therefore, not to recruit more of my country men, my brothers, who do not know the cause of your fight, who indeed, have nothing

6. Until 1920, Jubaland was administered as a part of the British East Africa Protectorate. In that year Britain ceded it to Italian Somaliland in part payment for Italy's intervention against the Germans during World War I. Mwase presumably refers to Chilembwe's protest against the employment of Nyasas in the various campaigns against the "Mad Mullah" in Northern Somaliland. Nyasas were also employed in a British war against the Ashanti.

7. They were recruited primarily as carriers, not soldiers.

to do with it as they have already shed their blood in different wars when recruited by you, yet they are not regarded as men of any value before you. It is better to recruit White Planters, Traders, Missionaries and other white settlers in the country, who are, indeed, of much value and who also know the cause of this war, and have something to do with it. But not to recruit a black man of this country who has nothing to do with it.[8]

This letter was written sometime in October 1914, for insertion in the Nyasaland Times. Andack [Jamali], one of his Office Clerk, took the letter, on a push cycle ⟨bicycle⟩, to the Editor, Nyasaland Times, Blantyre. After a day or so, Andack went again to Blantyre to see if it was inserted and to bring the paper. The paper was brought to John at 8 a.m. The words [that] were written in the paper ⟨a letter from the editor⟩ were as follows: "John Chilembwe, Your letter has been refused by the Censor." And at the foot of same, the Editor noted something about the Dutch request, which was also refused by the Government somewhere in South Africa, or where I cannot recollect.[9] After reading this paper sometime at 9 a.m. of the same morning, a runner came on a push cycle from Blantyre, said he was sent by the Editor of Nyasaland Times, to whom the runner was working,

8. This apparently is a paraphrase of Chilembwe's much longer letter, quoted in full by Shepperson and Price, *Independent African,* 234–236, and in part by Rotberg, *Rise of Nationalism,* 82–83. It was published in the initial runs of the *Nyasaland Times* of 26 November 1914, but deleted by the censor from all of the copies of that issue that were distributed to the public. The newspaper was then published weekly.

9. George Shepperson suggests that this mention of a "Dutch request" may be a garbled reference to the South African rebellion of 1914 that was led by Col. Salomon Maritz and General Christiaan Rudolf De Wet. For the date of Chilembwe's letter, its censorship, and the role of the editor, see Shepperson and Price, *Independent African,* 470–471; Rotberg, *Rise of Nationalism,* 83.

to tell John "to hide the paper, ⟨i.e., the letter⟩ and not to show it when Boma officials come to enquire about it, and said, his master, the Editor, is arrested, for inserting words about you John." [10] The paper was then hidden as requested. John called the chiefs and headmen and all eldermen of Mlanje, and around the Chiradzulu, and explained to them that was the reply to the request sent. Before John wrote this letter to the Editor, he first gathered up the chiefs, headmen and men ⟨elders⟩ for their advice. They unanimously asked John to write a letter and request as it was requested above. After receiving this paper and its words, and to learn that their request was not looked at [favorably], they were all sorry and nothing to say.

On 3rd December, a meeting was called up again to try to think what way they should do. Nothing definitely was then concluded. They went each man his way home. Sometime in the same month, another meeting was called up again, by John; all the chiefs etc. gathered up again, and begun to suggest their ideas. They all came to conclusion, that by not answering us on our request, means death on us. They all said that "It was better for all of us to die, than to live and see all these troubles, especially, to our women and children, whenever the husband is killed, leaving wife and children nothing in the kind of help such as pension or gratuity is given them, and after all they look very poor and useless.["] By this time, they all said that they should hold a last meeting again, in which to decide finally, and do the dead ⟨deed⟩, or else leave it for good.

10. The report of the arrest apparently was erroneous. The quotation marks in this sentence are as Mwase placed them.

On 3rd of January 1915 another meeting was held, and this was last of all. They all decided "to strike a blow," or else they should ask to be buried alive alternately. John referred to the meeting, something about one a Mr. John Brown of America, who after losing his hope, in succeeding the request in writing, to the authority concerned, in regard slave trading he determinate to strike a blow and lose his own life, than, as he said, [it] was too good for him and was ["]out of sight and reach." John said, this case stands the same as that of a Mr. John Brown, I have referred to above. "Let us then strike a blow and die," for our blood will surely mean something at last. They all came to a final conclusion of *"Let us strike a blow and die."*

Every man then went home with idea of preparing his weapon of any kind for the dead ⟨deed⟩. It was arranged that letters will be sent out, from the headquarters to all branches, who were the members of that counsel ⟨council⟩ or conspiracy—I cannot say which of the two—which letters will tell them the day, date and time, when the "blow" begun. Philip Chinyama of Dzunje, Ncheu District, was also consulted. He visited the headquarters personally, in November, and heard all about [the plans]. He also took a leadership for the Ncheu expedition, and went back after staying three weeks at the headquarters, at Chiradzulu. He was told that a letter would be sent to him for directions, the same letter will also tell him what day, date and time of "striking the blow" and then at last ["]die." [11]

11. Filipo Chinyama, an Ngoni, was a Seventh Day Baptist preacher who had been influenced by Joseph Booth. At heart he, like Charles Domingo and Chilembwe, was a religious rebel who had on several occasions aroused governmental antagonism and fears.

Sometime, [I] cannot remember the date in January 1915, John sent letters out to all members around. One was sent to Philip Chinyama by two runners. They were instructed to walk day and night and reach Chinyama's village by Friday of that very week. The instructions in all the letters were to tell the members to strike the "blow" on Saturday the 23rd January at 7 p.m. The same date, day and hour, was also at Mlanje, Chiradzulu and Blantyre. He divided divisions and sections. He promoted ⟨appointed⟩ some Majors and Captains etc. and placed them according to their sections and so on. John himself was then a Field Marshal of the whole Campaign.

The letter to Philip Chinyama of Ncheu was delivered late, as understood.[12] He was then arrested before striking the "blow" and was executed. Others of his forces were openly shot by a volley and killed. Philip received the letter of instructions on Saturday the 23rd January at 3:30 p.m. He called up a meeting of his force, on the morning of Sunday the 24th January. They were all surrounded by the Police force, from the [Ncheu] Boma, sent by the Resident, who received the informations by the wire, what had happened, the previous night at Chiradzulu by John and his force, soon the information again reached the Resident at Ncheu, that Philip was also mobilising his force against Ncheu Boma, and that they were still discussing the matter, in their Church.[13] Some

12. "As understood" could mean either that the letter was delivered later than planned or late according to Mwase's understanding.

13. Since the rebels had cut the wires between Blantyre and Zomba, a telegraph message could not have reached Ncheu until late on 24 January. Indeed, Claude Algernon Cardew, the then Resident at Ncheu, apparently learned of Chinyama's plans from several Principal Headmen who lived in the Livulezi valley. Once apprised, Cardew persuaded Njobvualema, an important Ngoni

of Philip's members were sentenced to death, by hanging, some to life [imprisonment], and others to certain number of years, by imprisonment.

So that divisional force was dispensed, before striking the blow; John's intention was to instruct Philip, to mobilise his divisional force on Saturday morning, and strike the "blow" on the Ncheu Boma at 7 p.m. the same evening. Philip would lead the sectional force in Liwonde and part of Portuguese East Africa near the boundary, [of] Ncheu and Portuguese East Africa. Mind you, Philip has some members ⟨followers⟩ in the Portuguese East Africa also. The assault would [be] continued from Ncheu on to Dedza[14] on the right wing, while the left wing would carry their assault towards the Liwonde, with extension to Neno, and meet imperial forces of John somewhere in the Matope, Blantyre District, while the right wing of the imperial forces was to assault the Zomba Planters and all in vicinity. A blockade was then put on by the information immediately received at Ncheu, in regard the instructions received by Philip.[15]

The other instructions issued out to other forces, I will describe them separately, as I wish to explain the whole matter clear enough, rather than to intermix them, and then make the readers misunderstanding the points and aims thereon. I am writing this

---

nduna whose area included the Kirk Range, to send out a warrior group to intercept Chinyama's followers. Meanwhile Cardew sandbagged the *boma*. In the event, Ian Nance says, "it seems that the party which went out to intercept the Chinyama gang persuaded them to surrender without a fight, and to give themselves up at the Boma." This report of conversations with Cardew is contained in a letter from Ian Nance to the editor, 3 July 1963.

14. But Dedza is north of Ncheu.

15. The meaning of this sentence is unclear. Did the *boma* or the Government mount a blockade? Did his instructions fall into British hands? What kind of a blockade? The official records do not allow us to clarify or to corroborate this very interesting allusion.

with great care, so that the reader will follow the whole matter properly [rather] than to be puzzled with it. Now I must describe how other forces were divided into sections.

First I must speak about the letter which was sent to Mlanje division. This letter was also delivered late and nothing was then done by that divisional force. Who was the leader of Mlanje division, I cannot remember his name, [but] there was also a big force formed there, for the same purpose.

The other forces were divided as follows: First Battalion was placed on Macheleni section under Johnstone [Zilongola] as Major, Jonathan Chigwinya and Lifeyo Chekacheka as Captains. Second Battalion to Magomero under Wilson Zimba as Major, Abraham Chimbiya as Captain. Third Battalion to Nsoni under Captain John Gray. Scout Major Duncan Kunjilima was placed in Blantyre Town. Another battalion under David Kaduya as Major, Stephen Mkulichi and C. Wallace Kampingo as Captains, was despatched to Blantyre specially for A.L.C. ⟨African Lakes Corporation⟩ Mandala Stores, for the purpose of seizing weapons, rifles, guns, cartridges and ammunition.[16]

Now I take first the battalion under Jonathan Chi-

16. Johnstone Zilongola had previously been the foreman of a road gang. John Gray Kufa Mapantha (Mapantha appears as his surname in Zomba archives file S 2/68^1/19) was a medical dispenser of some repute who worked on the Bruce estate. He was executed for his part in the rising. Njilima (the "Ku" here was a prefix of respect symbolizing property-owning status) was comparatively wealthy by local standards. He ran his own estate. Mkulichi was a teacher. (Mwase or his copyist misspelled the name throughout as Nkulichi.)

This would have been the logical place in the text to quote Chilembwe's instructions to the army on the morning of Saturday, 23 January 1915, but Mwase reserved it for his next chapter. The editor decided against rearranging Mwase's narrative, but some readers may wish to read those instructions now (p. 48) and then take up the story again here.

gwinya, who begun his assault on white Planters on
the upper Mombezi river, a second battalion under
Wilson Zimba begun their assault at the headquarters
of the Magomero Estates. A third battalion under
Captain John Gray of Nsoni broke the promise, the
Captain then shrinked, and did not do as they arranged at their headquarters, that he, John Gray, was
to begin his assault on the Nsoni Planters. He had
500 men strong. After John Gray shrinked all the
members of his battalion scattered away and diminished. Now Scout Major Duncan Kunjilima, [who] was
scout for Blantyre Township, shrinked also. The instructions given him at the headquarters was for him
to wait in Blantyre Town. He had 12 Askari who
were under the Resident at the Boma and who came
to an arrangement that they were to fall in as soon
[as] the battalion arrives at Mandala and as soon [as]
they will hear a sound of gun firing, they will come
up for help. Duncan Kunjilima then, with few men
would attack the Boma buildings, by setting fire to it.
He was supplied 4 tins of paraffin ⟨kerosene⟩ for
that purpose.

Now the last battalion under David Kaduya, Stephen Mkulichi and C. Wallace Kampingo, took their
directions towards Limbe Town. After arriving at
Limbe in the night, say about 9 p.m. they sat down
waiting the arrival of John Gray's battalion, for the
arrangement given to John Gray was to begin his
attack on the Nsoni [,to go] on to Midima and then meet
the battalion of David Kaduya at Limbe. As I have
already said that John Gray shrinked, and made no
movement. The battalion of David Kaduya waited a
great deal at Limbe and there was no sign of John
Gray's coming. At the very late in the night, David

Kaduya moved his battalion of 200 men strong on to the Blantyre town. They arrived at Mandala General Store, there the battalion was divided into three and surrounded the building. The native watchman, who, after explaining to him the full reason of their actions, and that they had no intention of attacking their fellow country men, but only whitemen, he kept shouting "Nkhondo! Nkhondo! (war war) [and] was shot dead at the spot. The store was then broke into by the front door, rifles and guns were taken out; while David himself broke the ammunition store and took out boxes of ammunition. One whiteman fired a shot once, he did this in his house. Now the battalion watched to see, if Duncan Kunjilima had done as instructed. Nothing was seen. The Askari who arranged to come up for help, some did come. This was then late in the morning, say about 4 a.m. These Askari were afraid to fall in, went back without helping. The battalion returned to Chiradzulu [and] met other battalions that of Majors Wilson Zimba and Johnstone, near Ndirande hill. Four men of this battalion of David were caught by the Boma Askari from Blantyre when following them, one of the men caught was Chimpere, a uterine [brother] of John Chilembwe. They were all killed by a volley on the next day. The three battalions then returned back to Chiradzulu on Sunday morning, the 24th of January.

At the headquarters, Andack and Burnett Kadango were placed in charge, John Chilembwe and all the women were put out from the headquarters at ⟨on⟩ a hill called Chilimangwanje. They were out of gun shot. Isaac Chambo, Sailes [?], Edison Chafunya and Morris Chilembwe, nephew of John, were with John and the women, at that hill.[17] The whole regiment promised that

17. The hill called Chilimangwanje is situated near Mbombwe,

does not matter what will happen, we shall come to fetch
you from here. If not here, you must be at Tuchila [or]
Machemba, or at Chisitu in the Portuguese East Africa.

When all battalions returned on the Sunday, John
came from the hill [where] he was, to receive information how far the army have fought and what was the
casualty to his army's side. He was told that white
women were brought in and children and also that
certain Planters were killed, and one head cut off
from a Planter was brought in also.[18] He then sent
some breads and other kind of food to the white
women who were kept at Harrison's House. He also
encouraged his army to be brave enough and die
intrepidly for the love of the country and country
men. He also told them about "Acerrema Proximorum
odia." [19] He meant to tell them that among the whitemen, there are your own relatives,[20] who will also
fight against you, and which is more better than to
be fought only by the strangers. He also told his
army that through Amor Patria, and Anirio et fide,
Fight on, fight on![21] Do not be discouraged by anything you see. I know you are only mean people

where Chilembwe had erected his church. In response to a specific
inquiry, Mr. Willie Chokani, sometime Malawi Minister of Labour
and Member of Parliament for Chiradzulu, informed the editor
that there were no traditions extant that connected Chilembwe with
Chilimangwanje. Nevertheless, Mwase's account could hardly have
been manufactured, particularly since the author knew the Chiradzulu district only generally. Edison Chafunya may have been
Fred Chifunya, a pupil in Chilembwe's main school.

18. The head of William Jervis Livingstone.

19. *Acerrima proximorum odia*—"The bitter hatred of their neigh-
bors."

20. Some of Chilembwe's supporters had been born of white
fathers and African mothers.

21. *Amor patriae*—"love of country." *Anirio* probably is a typing
mistake for *Animo*, which makes the phrase read: "With spirit and
devotion."

who have no velocity weapons to stand against the heavy and strong army of the whitemen. I did not mean you to succeed and defeat whitemen, no, not at all, that is not my idea even when I am standing here now. This [action] is only a hint to the whitemen, that the way they treat our country men and women is to grieve the whole country, and on behalf of all our country people, we choose to die for them. He again reminded his army to remember his first orders, before they were sent out for actions, that they must not touch anybody's property of any kind, for they were not fighting for wealth but for Amor Patria.

At 4 p.m. he went back to the hill the same day. This was Monday the 25th January. In the evening of same Monday a small patrol was sent on to Nguludi [Mission] under Johnstone. They brought news that one French man, of the White Fathers [Roman Catholic] Mission, was grievously wounded by young men of his patrol. He said probably will die the very night or so.[22]

Another patrol on Saturday the 23rd January was sent to Chiradzulu Boma to break [into] the Boma, and take some more weapons. The Resident was away to the Blantyre town. The patrol met with some native Askari who, although they were of the same arrangement ⟨in agreement with the rebellion⟩ at first, they ⟨the Askari⟩ were against them and repulsed them without loss. They returned without getting any weapons from that Boma.

On Monday the 25th January the white women were sent back to Chiradzulu together with their children. Certain men were sent and carried them.

22. Shepperson and Price (*Independent African*, 301) think that Kaduya may have led this patrol.

After a short distance, they espied a white army coming, the men then told the white women that they were returning back. They came back and warned their army, that they have espied whitemen's army coming, and will reach the headquarters soon. As they were speaking, they looked the other side of the river. There they espied whitemen's army coming, and [it] crossed the river. This was about 8 a.m. on Monday. Soon after, fighting begun, by both armies. A little heavier casualties were inflicted by the rebels to the whitemen's army. The rebels having only four wounded,[23] David Kaduya, the Major of a battalion, was one of the wounded. The whitemen's army was driven back, who retreated towards Chiradzulu. The rebels did not pursue the whitemen's army. The whitemen's army leaving two killed and certain of them wounded on that particular fight. The rebels remained at their headquarters the whole day. In the afternoon they placed some sentries around their station.

On Tuesday morning the 26th the sentries reported that they have not espied anything, and no signs of enemies coming. This was another mistaken the sentries brought again to the headquarters. By this report from the sentries made the rebels' army to rely on it and stay loose. This time the whitemen's army passed by [the sentries] and went round by the left wing. They passed between the sentries and the hill called Chilimangwanje where John Chilembwe was. Suddenly the rebels were attacked from the left wing. This assault by the whitemen's army was severely which ⟨was severe. It⟩ immediately blown out and scattered the rebels in disorderly towards Chilimang-

23. The numbers are slightly different in *Independent African*, 297.

wanje hill. The rebels after arriving there, they found
John and the women were not at that place. They thought
he might have gone to Tuchila. They went there
and found no sign of John [or] even other men. They
went to Machemba [and found] no trace of John also
there. Then they went to Chiradzulu—another one in
the Portuguese East Africa—and then to Chisitu in the
Portuguese East Africa also, that was the place they
thought John might have been there, there was no
trace of John again. Then they returned to Mausi in
the Nyasaland again, that was the 1st day of February. John was not there. On the 2nd day of February
they went to a thick forest called Pyerepyere. There
also they failed to trace John's whereabouts. They
camped on the end of this forest, looking towards
Pyerepyere plain. They placed sentries other side
of the Dambo ⟨marsh⟩ and not behind them. They
thought our enemy would never come through the
thick forest, but they may come through by crossing
the Dambo. And they believed that their enemy will
not trace their whereabouts.

After camping there, they sent twelve men as scouts
on to Magomero. Twelve others to Tumbwe. Both
these scout patrols were instructed to come back and
report at the Camp on Thursday or Friday the same
week. The army was reduced to 50 men strong, after
sending out 24 scouts on duty. They waited there for
the scouts till Thursday, Friday, Saturday and Sunday. No sign of their coming. On Monday morning
one of their Captains, Wallace Kampingo, suggested
through his past night dream, that they should abandon the Camp and retreat for safety somewhere. He
said, I am sure those scouts are captured. Majors,
Wilson Zimba and others, rejected the suggestion which

was from a dream by Captain Wallace Kampingo.
Wallace Kampingo being a young man tho' promoted
Captain of a battalion, was too young for the bigger
men to take his suggestion or advice. Wallace, after
he was refused of his proposals, took up a patrol
across the Dambo, accompanied by one, Andrew Mkulichi, the younger brother of Captain Stephen Mkulichi. After returning from their patrol across the Dambo
back to the Camp, about quarter or so of an hour,
they were heavily fired on, from their backward, where
they did not expect their enemy to come through. It
was quite unexpectedly attack on them. They all aban-
doned the Camp in disorderly. None of them picked
up his rifle, except Stephen Mkulichi, who was wounded
just as he ran and killed. At the Camp two were
killed, Captain Stephen Mkulichi and Nelson Nyamu-
liwa. Wilson Zimba was wounded. The whole army
was in a full retreat towards the Dambo. Just after
crossing the Dambo, Captain Wallace was wounded
left leg and crippled. His boy ⟨servant⟩ helped him
by tieing a bandage round the leg but [he] was unable to walk further; was lying there. Two of his men
came to try to carry him on to the village, but were
unable to do so. Andrew Mkulichi was narrowly escaped, all his shirts he was wearing was all torn off
by bullets, but did not receive any wound in his
body. These two men who were killed were left on
their death places, the hyenas played their flesh the
whole night. Only the head of one, Stephen Mkulichi
was found the next morning and taken into Boma.
Wilson Zimba was carried into the Boma by the enemy, this was the end of the whole struggle.

After this, most of their members were captured
and brought to judgment. A great number were con-

demned to death by hanging on a scaffold and others were fired upon by a volley. Certain of them were sentenced to life. Majority to a certain number of years. Wallace Kampingo was the last Captain of them all. [Those] Captured at the end, who were condemned to death were all executed at the K.A.R. ⟨King's African Rifles⟩. [24] They all died bravely, singing hymns of their Great God when [they] were escorted towards a scaffold for their last time in the world.

24. The British-officered East African military forces. Battalions were recruited in Nyasaland, Kenya, and Uganda, and, in time of peace, based in the capital of each protectorate or colony.

When the army gathered on Saturday morning on the 23rd January 1915 [John Chilembwe gave instructions to his army]. After a long debate,[1] he prayed to Almighty God. Then he delivered his speech as follows:

"You are all patriots as you sit. Patriots mean[s] to die for Amor Patria. This very night you are to go and strike the blow and then die. I do not say that you are going to win the war at all. You have no weapons ⟨guns?⟩ with you and you are not at all trained military men even. One great thing you must remember is that Omnia Vincit Amor[2] so for love [of] your own country and country men, I now

1. About strategy and/or goals?
2. "Love conquers all." For some reason Mwase put "Omnia" in parentheses. It is very unlikely that John Chilembwe interspersed his speeches with Latin aphorisms. The Latinisms are probably Mwase's gloss, particularly since he seems consciously to have striven for literary effects. Mwase presumably derived his knowledge of Latin from his education by missionaries at Livingstonia. The Latin phrases and aphorisms that appear in the remainder of the text are notably corrupt—in some cases almost indecipherable. Nevertheless, they reflect Mwase's love of the grand gesture, his desire to impress his readers with superior learning and, of course, an ability to turn to his own use the mannerisms and knowledge of white men. In general, his text imparts a Biblical flavor and, despite the weird syntax and crude grammar of the original, Mwase employs a surprisingly rich English vocabulary in view of the probability that English was his third language after Tonga and Nyanja.

48

encourage you to go and strike a blow bravely and die.

"This is only way to show the whitemen, that the treatment they are treating our men and women was most bad and we have determined to strike a first and a last blow, and then all die by the heavy storm of the whitemen's army. The whitemen will then think, after we are dead, that the treatment they are treating our people is almost ⟨most⟩ bad, and they might change to the better for our people. After we are dead and buried. This blows means 'non sibi sed patria.' [3]

"You must not think that with that blow, you are going to defeat whitemen and then become Kings of your own country, no. If one of you has such an idea in his head, 'God forbid,' he must throw such idea now, before it grows bigger in his head, for it will lead him astray. I am also warning strongly against seizing property from anybody, does not matter what or where. If among you there is a lecher, such a man must not go with you. You are Patriots and not Lechers. Where you are going to find money, goods and other kind of wealth, does not matter what, do not touch such for 'Amor Patria' sake. But where ever your hand is going to lay on any kind of a weapon, take that, for it will help you in your struggle for the 'Amor Patria.' Another order I want you to remember, is about women and young children, do not, in any way, do anything to them, treat them as innocents, what you are to do with them is to bring them over peacefully, and afterwards send them back to the Boma. Women must be carried on Machilla if some will be available. If some of the whitemen will

3. *Non sibi sed patriae*—"Not for oneself but for one's country."

49

be killed during the assault, one or two of the important men bring the head or heads over, leave the body alone."

He repeated saying "Be of good courage, and strike the blow and die for the 'Amor Patria,' and not with intention to win and become Kings of your own." He bade them "God's speed." At last he prayed again and said "Deusvobiscum." [4]

So the army scattered that day for their food. This was the morning of Saturday the 23rd January. The army then gathered themselves, at the evening, and they were divided as I have already said on the front page ⟨earlier⟩. I have also to mention that there were also some members of this army in Zomba Township, but they all shrinked and diminished, and they did not appear for help; although the arrangement was that.

4. A Baptist preacher would be unlikely to dismiss his flock with *Deus vobiscum* ("God be with you"). The Latin is probably Mwase's, not Chilembwe's.

● CHILEMBWE'S LETTER WRITTEN
TO THE GERMANS

I have already said how the rebels were dispersed and their army was put to flight and perished. Now I want to speak about the letter which John wrote and sent on to the Germans to German East Africa (now Tanganyika Territory). This letter was written on Sunday the 24th of January, when he, John, was at Chilimangwanje Hill. The words of the letter I cannot tell what was written in.[1] Commonly [it was said that] it was written to inform the Germans that he had also attacked the English men [on] this side, and asking them of their assistance. He wanted them to come up from German East Africa by the Malokotera ⟨?⟩ in Portuguese East Africa into Nyasaland, and join his army. He thought his army would stand longer against their foe. This letter was sent by two men, one of the men was Yotam Bangwe ⟨Bango⟩. This letter was taken over to the Germans, who received it with much pleasure, and proposed to come to Nyasaland, to meet John's army somewhere in Nyasaland or near about, and then help him to fight the English men.[2] This man Yotam did not return, but was caught

1. Neither the original nor copies have ever been found.
2. As far as we know, the Germans simply replied in general terms, promising encouragement only. See Robert I. Rotberg, "Resistance and Rebellion in British Nyasaland and German East Africa, 1888–1915," in *Britain and Germany in Africa,* ed. Prosser Gifford and William Roger Louis (New Haven, 1967), 688–689.

sometime in 1919 by the Nyasaland Government and was put to prison. The Germans after receiving informations from John, tried to come into Nyasaland by the Malokotera [in] Portuguese East Africa. They were then repulsed with a heavy loss, and were forced to retreat.[3]

As I have already stated that John was not found in any places they had arranged with him to be. He unfortunately went to Mlanje, where it was understood, was met by the whitemen's army, was shot and killed; and then buried there. His nephew Morris Chilembwe, who was in his company, was also shot and killed, and buried at Machemba not by his uncle John near the Boma at Mlanje.[4] This was the end of everything.

3. These actions seem not to have occurred. The narrative returns to the German problem later. See 59–66.

4. John Chilembwe was apparently buried in an unmarked grave about two miles from the Mlanje *boma*.

Now I want to follow their ⟨the rebels'⟩ last Captain,
Wallace Kampingo, who was wounded and crippled
when running at the Pyerepyere Dambo. I have already said that he was lying there in the forest with
his boy. Later in the same day, two men of their
members ⟨fellow rebels⟩ came, and carried him towards a village. At 10 p.m. they arrived at the Nyuku
tree (Fig tree) about 6 miles to a village. The two
men left him there with his boy; went to look for
their wives and [said] that they would return back
to the place soon. These men before they went a
distant of about 6 miles further, they were captured
by the enemy. So they did not return as they promised.
Next morning, Wallace give 2/- to his boy, to go to
a village and buy food for both of them; the boy
went away with the 2/- towards a village but never
returned. He left his jacket and a piece of lona
⟨stout, waterproof cloth⟩ there.

Wallace stayed under the fig tree alone for four
days without food, but water was close by, where
he kept going after it and deep in his leg into the
water, for it was very much swollen, and would not
walk or stand up. On the fifth day, one man came
under that tree, and saw Wallace lying there. He
asked him what was the matter with his leg; Wallace
then told the man the whole story. The man, who

53

was an Anguru descendant, went away towards where he came from, soon after, he brought two cooked pumpkins and give them to Wallace. He then went away again back to his village and did not come again.

On the sixth day Wallace thought to try and walk slowly towards a village, which he did. He arrived at a village at 10 p.m. and gave ordinary "Odi" to a house.[1] There came out a man, who asked him who was he; Wallace then told him who he was, and all about. This man said that he was a brother-in-law of one Burnett Kadango, who was one of their men ⟨the rebels⟩.[2] He then took him into his hut, and prepared a soft gruel for him. In the morning about 5 a.m. he took him into the bush. He spent two days there; the third day the man arranged with other people to carry him to Cholo, where Wallace thought to go to his brother. Wallace told the man who carried him, that he would pay them when arriving at his brother at Cholo. They carried him on the piece of lona which was left by his boy. This was some time in the night. They brought him to a village in the middle of a night, the headman of

1. *Odi*, or *Hodi*, is an originally Swahili greeting now common in Malawi and Zambia; it corresponds roughly to "Hello. May I come in?" The Nguru, or Lomwe, began occupying sections of the Shire Highlands in the late nineteenth century. See C. Baker, "A Note on Nguru Immigration to Nyasa," *Nyasaland Journal*, XIV, 1 (1961), 41–42; Thomas Price, "The Name 'Anguru,'" *ibid.*, V, 1 (1952), 23–25.

2. After serving a sentence in prison, Burnett or Barnet Kadango (d. 1963/4) joined the African civil service and finished his career as an Executive Officer in the Zomba *boma*. Ian Nance recalled that Kadango was "a charming old man who acted as wet nurse to many generations of assistant district commissioners. He would tell one that he had been imprisoned for his part in the Chilembwe affair but would never open up at all to what his part had been." Nance, letter to the editor, 18 September 1965.

that village, who was an Anguru descendant, asked these carriers who they were carrying; and where they were going with the person they were carrying. They told him who he was and where they were taking him. The headman then warned the carriers that, if you continue carrying him, and if you are to be captured by the whitemen, and found you carrying this man, you are all to be killed by the whitemen together with the man you are carrying. These men then, they were discouraged and instead of carrying him on, they took him into a thick bush, and leave him there. They did not come back. This was at the middle of the night.

Wallace then remained at the place for three days without food, but water was about there, so he kept washing his wounds. On the fourth day he thought to walk slowly on towards a village. He came to a road which led him to a village. He then left off the road and went into the edge of a garden. His leg swollen up very much [more] than it was, and [he] was lying there for some time. Later on, an old woman happened to pass there, and she saw him. She asked him where was he coming from, and what was the matter with his leg. Wallace then told her all about. She went away and brought back some kind of food and gave it to him, but he could not eat it, the throat was also swollen. She then shouted for men, men came up and begun to question him, he told them all about. So the men arranged to carry him to the village. They did so. They reported to their village headman who advised them to carry him on. They brought him to a white Planter at Midima. The white Planter, whom his name was not known to him, addressed his wound and provided his own Machilla, also a letter was given to the carriers for the Boma at Blantyre. These men carried him on to Mikalongwe Station and was put in a train for Blantyre. After arriving Blantyre Boma, was put in prison, his wound was attended to at the Government Dispensary. Later on he was sent to Zomba. This was the end of the last Captain, who was afterwards sentenced to life imprisonment with hard labour.

I have, therefore, explained fully of everything now, for the public to know and understand. First I have dug out John's birth place and what his tribe, where his grandparents came from, where he first been educated, where he received good education and who took him there, the time when he came back from America. The time he started his Mission at Chiradzulu, his behaviour towards his members and all around Chiradzulu and outside Chiradzulu, how the people regarded him; what made him to mobilise an army and rebel against his Government, and what orders he issued out to his army before they went for a blow. I have dig out everything clearly.

Now I want to state what happened to all women who were with John himself at Chilimangwanje Hill. John when he saw fire set on the houses, at his headquarters, he knew that his army was no longer exist. He then wrote a letter addressed to the Captain in charge of the whitemen's forces, and gave it to one, Isaac Chambo, one of his Sergeant Majors. He instructed him to take letter and all the women back. He gave him a white flag. Isaac Chambo then took the women towards their station. At a distant of three miles. Isaac was met by a patrol of Askari, under two whitemen, who were in a pursuit of the scattered rebels. He lifted the flag high for the patrol to see it. Immediately he was captured and was tied against a tree ready for a volley. One of the two whitemen was behind, and when he came found the other whitemen has already ordered the Askari to get ready to fire a volley on Isaac, who was tied standing against the tree. He, the whiteman, asked what was the matter about him. The other whiteman showed the letter which Isaac had brought written by John. The other whitemen read the letter and then asked Isaac, where John was; Isaac said he had not seen John personally, but that this letter was given to those women, and that he only met them a little time past. So the women asked me ⟨Chambo⟩ to lead them to you, therefore, here am I. All this time the women were standing by, trembling. The two whitemen begun to talk by themselves for a while. Afterwards the whiteman who came after the other, gave order to the Askari to untie Isaac off from a tree. He was then untied, and was told that from that time he was a prisoner. He was then captured and taken back to the whitemen's Camp; from there to the K.A.R. Zomba ⟨the King's African Rifles encampment in Zomba⟩. Isaac was then sentenced to a term of imprisonment. The women were sent back to their villages after giving their evidence in the court. Among the women—Mrs. John Chilembwe was with them, and she was also brought at the K.A.R. and afterwards was sent back to her village.

I am very sorry to have omitted one Captain Johnstone, who, after his battalion was put to a disorderly retreat, he crossed the border with few men of his battalion into Portuguese East Africa. Some time after he was there, it was then reported to the Portuguese Authority that the scattered rebels have crossed the border [and] are settling in. They were then arrested and sentenced to a term of imprisonment by the Portuguese Law. They were very lucky that none of them was shot or killed by hanging. After they finished their terms, they returned back to their home, with the exception of Johnstone who settled there for good after his release.

Now, I am sure, that I have gone so far much with the matter. What remains now, is to think over upon the whole thing, and put an opinion on the matter. This requires more better head to suggest such opinion. As the matter lies open like that, for someone to put his opinions, I voluntarily take up the risk of entering in what I think it would have been done. I do not mean I am correct.

● REMARKS ON LETTER SENT TO THE GERMANS

"Pace tua." [1] I wish to remark something. Before I do so, I must remember that the Liberty of the press does not mean to write things which would harm other people, whether white or black. The thing I want to remark first, is about the letter, which was sent to the Germans for help. This letter was to call the assistance of the Germans, who, I am sure, if they should be able to come to that help, or if would be possible defeat the English men, they could be the Superiors in the country. On the first place I must say that, John was not aware of the German Laws. If he was aware of the German Laws and Regulations, surely he would have not written the letter to them, asking them of their alliance. I, the writer of this book, [had] been in German East Africa (which is now called Tanganyika Territory) before the war, and had a good study of the German Laws and Regulations. Have also been in Portuguese East Africa, and studied their one sided Laws and Regulations as well. In my opinion, and if I were John, surely, I could never communicated with the Germans nor the Portuguese in the respect of "Commune Corum." [2] From what I have seen, I do not call that nation,

1. Literally "peace be with you," but here "by your leave."
2. Reading *coram* for *corum*, this phrase probably means "publicly or privately."

Germans, but I call them in Arabic, "Hamsa-eshilin," with interpretation of "Twenty-five." [3] They are very cruel, for a very small matter they flog, not less than twenty-five [times]. They do not like to take evidence in Court carefully, word by word as the English men usually do. Perhaps they do so only between white to white only, as I did not attend the cases arose between white to white. What I am commenting, are the native cases. Any word a chief has said, or told to do, to his men, or women, does not matter how bad it stands, that must be observed. If one will put an argument, that person will be flogged twenty-five. As soon ⟨As often as not?⟩ the chief will report not to take his evidence at all, they were only to satisfy ⟨the Germans?⟩ with the words, on the evidence of the chief or Jumbe (Headman) and in many cases "Hamsa-eshilin" was always to be inflicted on their black subjects. Most of their black subjects called them Hamsa-eshilin now and then. I heard a lot of their black subjects complaining, even some of them nearly to evacuate the territory for safety in English Territories. But they said that, they could not leave the Germans although they were cruel, for three good reasons.

(1) That the Germans were not imprisoning the life of a person, as the English men often do, to sentence a person to life. They said that was timidy ⟨??⟩ even the Germans themselves were frequently telling their black subjects that, "beware of an English man, he is imprisoning life of person." The Germans were not putting person in prison more than five years for a big case. And for a very bad criminal

3. That is, twenty-five lashes. The word is apparently a corruption of the Arabic *Khamsa wa* (colloq. *wi*) *'ishirin,* commonly used for "twenty-five" on the East African coast. Up-country speakers of Swahili now prefer *ishirini na tano.*

case, such a person, if found guilty of malicious murder, was to be condemned to death and fire a volley on him or her. Homicide and manslaughters were to be sentenced not more than five years.

(2) They did not put a restriction on their subjects with regard in buying guns and rifles—a black subject could have as many weapons he may like to possess, and no restriction on his shooting game as long [as] he can bring over the tusks which were lying on the ground to the Government as loyalty.[4]

(3) That they were not in habit of sending out Capitãos or Askari in the villages for the purpose of collecting taxes, or writing names of people as Census, for the purpose of tax. Their methods of collecting taxes were through the Sultans and Jumbe. Each Jumbe had to tell the number of people he had in his village. The tax receipts were to be given to him equal to the number of his people. He was then to collect the money from his people himself, and issue the receipts as he collected the money. The Jumbe then was to bring the money into the Boma. If there would be a deficit the Jumbe was told to make it up, either in cash or in kind. In kind, they meant, the Jumbe would go out, hunting elephants, and bring some tusks in lieu of cash, and squares the deficit.

So, I am sure without the three reasons above mentioned, the "Hamsa-eshilin" people would have lost a great number of their black subjects.

The Portuguese are the people who can put a person on remand in prison without hearing the case,

4. Traditionally, all "ground" tusks of an elephant belonged to the sovereign of the area in which the elephant had been shot. See below, p. 126.

sometimes four or five years, and afterwards when hearing the case, found him or her not guilty or found him guilty and sentence him to two months or so. They often take evidence from the first person ⟨the plaintiff⟩, does not matter what kind of lies the first person has spoken; they take it as enough evidence to convict or remand the second person in prison.

John in his speech, which he delivered to his meeting, he said that the treatment my country men and women were receiving was almost ⟨most⟩ unpleasant. He said they were illtreatment by the white Planters and other whitemen in the country. Did John expected his people to receive better treatment from the Germans? What kind of good treatment would be expected from them? Do you not think that the treatment from the Germans would be more ⟨worse⟩ than the former? Yes, no doubt of that indeed. That should be a very big mistake, if the Germans would, by the invitation of John, by that letter, came up, and conquer the country. Their cruel Laws and Regulations would be a very heavy yokes on our weak necks. This would probably cause to form another great contest, either among the country men themselves or against the Germans, either of which I cannot possibly state. From the view of the fact the whole state of affairs would then turn terribly. Because, no person can better himself by cutting his nose. John's idea, to invite an alliance with the Germans, or Portuguese, would meant to cut the nose of the country. No [one] can look better with a nose cut. His idea, from his own speech, to the audience, said, "The whitemen are treating my country men and women almost ⟨most⟩ bad." Yet he wrote a letter of invitation to the Germans. Were the Germans black-men?

Is it possible for a person to say, that, I do not like to wear a blue suit, because it looks black, and yet he goes to a draper, and ask the draper to make him a black suit? Where is the difference? May I say that such a person is a person who does not like to wear blue stuff? No, I will not, unless I am a fool of the very greatest size. But, if I see him go to the draper and ask a khaki or a white suit to be made for him, then I will agree to what he will tell me that he does not like to use black suit. Certainly, this would have made more serious feelings among the country men. The Germans would have brought their heavy yoke, which neither John nor anyone else would . . . . ⟨have liked?⟩ it.[5] The quarrel between relatives or between the country men could have been grown tremendously. How far it will sound well to your ears, if one will tell you that he is able to rescue a prey from a leopard and then throw it to the lion's mouth? Is that to rescue the prey? Will you call such as a person of sound [mind]? and not insure ⟨insane⟩? Mind you, I do not mean that John was . . . . . . ⟨unsound⟩ no, certainly John was of sound mind, and sober all his life time.

But what he meant about this no one can tell out; only he himself knew what he meant and nobody else. As I have stated that the freedom of press does not mean to write words or things which are harmful to other people or to the country itself. What I have written about John's mistakes, I do not mean

5. The row of dots suggests that a typist could not read Mwase's writing.

to harm his name at all. This is an opinion from my own head, and it is easy for my head to make an equal mistake [to that] which John, though highly educated, did make. This is purely Sine Odio, but "Pro bono publico." [6] Do not then think that I have commented these words against John, no, but against the error created. For it would have been "tent pis," [7] if the Germans would come over, and then took over the country from the British. Who could stand the Germans' Law? Who could stand Hamsa-eshilin? Do you think to enjoy your country means to own different kind of velocity weapons?

Beside this, the German Territory lacked very much of better Schools. 95 percent of German Schools were Roman Catholic Schools, which, we all know, that Roman Catholic Schools are the last weak ⟨weakest?⟩ Schools ever been in our country.[8] I do not mean that they are bad Schools, but I say they are weak, in teaching high standards.

They ⟨the Catholics⟩ are, indeed, very good preachers, of course, good preaching is indeed required because it gives a person a confidence for the reward of Heaven. But who can tell of this Heavenly reward? No person in the world can describe how big, long deep wide or how many lbs. in weight. Therefore, it is good for a person, while waiting the heavenly glory, do something which, will make him to satisfy, that as the earth produces such fruits, the heavenly fruits as gift to me, will be much plenty, then I

6. "Without hatred, but for the public good."
7. He means *tanto peius*—"so much worse," or the French *tant pis*, "just too bad."
8. In 1930, Nyasaland had 2,685 schools attended by about 73,000 Africans. Two Roman Catholic orders ran about 1,000 of these schools.

enjoy the fruits of the earth.[9] [There is] no living person who knows what kind of reward he is to receive from heaven, or at arrival in heaven. Mind you, do not take me to be atheist, but take me as theist, and as a person of the Christian faith. The reward of heaven is a very simple question, that even a baby in Religion may answer it ten thousand times or more. For instance, if you ask a child today, what does he expect to receive from heaven, if he does well, he will eloquently say that, reward and gifts from God. And if you ask him, how big long, wide or heavy is the reward or gifts? he will never reply that. Therefore to educate a scholar in materially and in divine knowledge, is the most. Education in materially will keep him of the present life. Which is also valuable, just alike with the other one, which he expect to receive as a reward from Heaven. Of course, the heavenly life is immortal, while the earthly one is mortal. But as a poetry say, the little you have on hand values twice, the one you only expect.

I do not mean that I am against the Roman Catholic Religion. They are very kind people than any other Missionaries in the country. They show real love towards everyone. They can eat and chat together with anybody without respect of colour. I will [be] very sorry, if some of my remarks, will cause other people feel when reading them [that I was against the Roman Catholic religion], surely I did not mean it, if I meant it "Ruat Coelum" on me. As "hominis est errare," the same may apply to me, for which may be kindly apologised.[10] All this, I meant to show clearly

---

9. The commas in this involved sentence are Mwase's.

10. "May heaven crash down upon me," and "It is human to err."

the mistake created by John, by writing for an invitation alliance ⟨by inviting an alliance⟩ to the Germans, who were all round ⟨thoroughly?⟩ whitemen. I know, one will think that I have remarked this, because John is dead. No, indeed, if John was alive, I could certainly interviewed him personally on the subject, and probably I would give him a long debate. Beside that, I would be very pleased to found out from him the real idea of his writing this letter to the Germans and what he expected from them after they took over the country from the British if they were able to do so.

● HOW I THINK JOHN WAS LIKE WITH REGARD HIS DEPORTMENT

First, I must say that John was a person of high disposition, a benevolent man. Why I say this? I will certainly explain my reasons, which have given me such mind. Please watch me carefully on this explanation. If I am wrong, kindly check it off, out of your mind and thoughts. I am very sorry if my thoughts will lead other people astray, when trying to follow them. May I be pardoned for such please? On the front page ⟨earlier⟩, I have written that John had a great number of men to attend his meetings. The meetings he started in October, [continued] up to 3rd of January, the following year. I have said that he had members in Chiradzulu, Mlanje, Blantyre, Zomba, Liwonde and Ncheu and even in Portuguese East Africa. Some of Chiradzulu members, Blantyre members and Zomba members, were chiefs, headmen and the Boma or the Government Askari, who knew and heard all the long debates which conspicuously, was meant [to foment] a conspiracy against the whitemen who were in the country, who, John said, that they have deprived the freedom of our men and women. Yet these men, some of them, as I have said, were working under different whitemen but never dared to whisper to [one] of the whitemen they were working [for], nay, not one. Others were chiefs and headmen whose it was their duty to report to the

Government what was happening or which was likely to happen, in the near future. Some were Government Askari whose duty were to arrest the assembly before they could [go] any further with it. Neither of them did anything which could be as a signal to the whitemen, of what was to happen then.

These two reasons have led me to think that John was of high disposition, kind, benevolent and very popular man among his fellow country men, and women as well. For it is quite impossible for a man such as John was to suggest such idea, which meant great loss to property and especially lives, [and] that thousands of men could quickly accept it [even though] that meant that [they] accepted hazardous of their own lives, as well as the lives of others who were to implicate themselves in it. Yet they all took up the hazarding of their lives. I can say that no chief, [no matter] how big he would have been, would have suggested that fatal idea, [so] that people as I have mentioned from different districts, could take his mortal proposals, nay, none. Yea, before the word of such fatal speech finishes or leaving off his mouth he would have found himself already committed to prison, some people would have gone to report the ill proposals or conspiracy of the assembly at the scattering of the first meeting, or the Askari would bring the news of the conspiracy before the Boma [where] they were working, yet, none done so. What all the whitemen first knew, was the attack, and the blow struck, as it was arranged by them at their meeting. If all the members were his Church members then I would think differently. These chiefs, headmen, Philip Chinyama, and the Askari, were not of his Church members at all, but yet, they turned up with one heart, and mobilised an army. Surely, John must have been a very particular person, the people regarded his work to be of a heavy weight. Although they saw danger was in front of his word, or proposals, they never frightened to what would happen after accepting his idea or proposals. I am certain they knew beforehand that they were hazarding their lives, but as John proposals ⟨proposed⟩ it to them, they did not like to pay attention to what would happen hereinafter.[1] I cannot, indeed, describe what kind of a person John was, and how much weight he had in the minds of other people who saw him and heard his words. It is not always common to people to take grave advice from another, unless he is of opinion, that the person [who] advises him is of more value to him, otherwise he cannot follow it for an inch even.

Secondly, I take John as a Patriot. I know there will be some question why and how I know he was such a person. I will briefly explain why I call him a Patriot. I have already written and stated where John received his education.[2] He was taken by Mr. Booth to America, and was then put into a School or a College, I do not know which, for his education, where he was ordained to Pastorship. He then determined to return back to his country, leaving pleasures of all sorts in America, coming back to a poor country as this. America as far I am aware is the best country, where a Negro of Africa, such as John was, would permanently settle there, and enjoy the beauty of that country with his fellow Negroes. John was not delighted with the fat of the country, made up his

1. That is, since Chilembwe, whom they trusted, proposed revolt, the other conspirators refrained from questioning his wisdom and willingly accepted his line of reasoning.
2. See above, p. 22.

69

mind to return to his birth country. If I were I, surely I could never dream, after having a big fortune of reaching America, of returning to this country. I would never pay any attention whether the country was my birth country. Nor to think, even, to pay a short visit to my parents and relatives if I had any. As for the pleasures of America, to a Negro was far beyond than any other country on the world, as I am told, where a Negro has a better freedom, as that in America. Therefore John must have been a good Patriot, to think to abandon all such pleasures and come back to his birth land knowingly, that [in] the country was never had any liberty to a Negro, to enjoy for himself without being interfered with. He well knew the using of a hat by a Negro, in this country, at that time, near a whiteman, was to offend the whitemen and probably would be beaten, yet John took no notice of such worries. He decided to come back to his country.

I think you will agree with me that in that time of John was quite different time. Many things were opposed to, and even rejected, [by] any whitemen. Especially a Planter could make a law of his own, for a Negro to observe.[3] It was, indeed, totally different with the time we are in now, which look better enough. So John must have remembered his country tho' it was in an awful state. He had love towards his country, and the country people. He thought the better education, which he himself had received, should be shared to his country people. He thought to tell

3. Mwase presumably means that the white planters made and enforced their own regulations with regard to the cutting of wood, the harvesting of crops, etc., on their own estates. Like the missionaries, they fined or flogged the laborers, who had little means of redress, or even knowledge of the possibility of redress.

them what he had seen among people of other country do.

How many people have emigrated to America from this country without returning back? I, the writer of this book, have lost two cousins, who have emigrated to that country some twenty-eight years ago, and I have even lost their whereabouts now. They do not like to return nor to write. Besides me, they have other important relatives, brothers and sisters, but through the better enjoyment of that country, they have checked out every thought in regard their relatives. I would be one of them, if I were with them there. Now look round, who was here? John. Was he not a funny young man? Clearly so. On that case, I call him a Patriot. John, before he went away to America, had no family of his own ⟨i.e., no nuclear family⟩. What made him to return here I wonder. His mother and father were both alive, they had other children to be looked after by them. Well, what made him to return? Love of his country and country people. All the heaps of pleasures were heaped for him in America, he looked at them as dunghill, so he returned.

Thirdly, John must have been a hero. Why? Yes, you are right to put why. I will tell you what I mean to say he was a hero. A hero means brave. I have already said that John mobilised an army against whitemen. I cannot tell how many people were mobilised for his army, it does not matter much to me. Now I want to tell you of his bravery. John knew the whitemen to be crafts. He again knew and see how big armies the whitemen had. He saw what a great number of velocity and strong weapons the whitemen had. How big stores of food [with] which to supply their army the whitemen had. How big was their money for which to employ a great number of people for their reinforcement. How great was their number. How strong their army was then. How big was the quantity of their medicines and drugs. How many Doctors and Dressers were to turn up to help their men. How many who could turn out as stretcher bearers, for the purpose of carrying away woundeds and deads from the fighting line into the Camp, for treatment.[4] He also knew how many will turn out as Surgeon Majors, Surgeon Captains for their men, and how many will turn out as porters. He also knew that the whitemen were military trained soldiers, and that their army also, does not matter black, ⟨i.e., the black soldiers included⟩ was trained army. They had also hospitals all around. They had building materials —if they come to a river on pursuing their enemies, they can construct a bridge and cross on. They had air machines to act against their enemies by dropping mortal bombs. And that they had different kind of ways to fight their enemy off their sight soon, if wanted to which were more dreadful, for a man like John, to venture to attack them, with, I do not know how many thousands of men.[5]

None of John's [men] was so cunning to lead the army. How small in number his army was. No weapons of any sort, except spears and assegai ⟨stabbing spears⟩, which would never reach their enemy from fifty yards. Bows and arrows which would be shot to a distant of hardly sixty yards. No stores of food for his army. No money for which to employ more men for reinforcement. How weak were men of his army

4. These are indications of Chilembwe's knowledge rather than questions.

5. This confusing sentence is rendered exactly as punctuated in the typescript.

to stand against strong army, no medicines or drugs of any kind. No Doctors and Dressers to attend the wounded men, no Surgeon Majors etc., and no porters to carry their food, weapons and the like, no hospitals where to treat the wounded. No air machine guns, which to fire on aeroplanes, when espied in the air, for the purpose of dropping bombs. No steamers and trains, for conveying his troops for reinforcement. In spite of all these dreadful weapons, and ways of fighting, John thought, and did strike a blow. Is he not a hero then? Follow me carefully please.

John when organising his troops at the first instance, he said, I want you to go and "strike a blow, and then die." He knew at the beginning that his idea of striking a blow on a whiteman meant his death: Death meant destruction of his own life and that of the other people who were to involve themselves in it. Death does not mean to enjoy at large at all, but decay and ruin, yet John hazarded it. Is that not though ⟨thought?⟩ heroic? If I were I, to reply that question I could eloquently say, yes, why? No person on the earth, unless is a very intrepid, can rise against a lion at his prey, equipped with a maize stalk, and attack the lion with it and depend upon pulling off the teeth, jaws, and claws from the lion himself, would [he] not be called hero?

John knew that whitemen have strong weapons, strong army and that they were trained, yet he went and struck them with a maize stalk. He depended that he would get weapons from the whitemen themselves, and fight them with their own weapons. Is this not absurd? Not only absurd, but wonderful intrepidity. By this time, John had family of his own to be instructed and look after, yet he proposed an

73

idea which, he knew and believed it was leading him to unspeakable ruin, from which, he was not at any time [sure] whether [he could] return and look after his family. He was aware that the result would be his mortality, and that he was not to enjoy the beauty of the country he was struggling about. But what was his profit to do such struggle? He wanted to win heroic, and nothing else. Has he won it? Clearly so. John was the first and last man to attempt to strike a whiteman with a maize stalk in this country. I cannot, of course, state what will be the state of affairs, after a century from now. That I leave it with our great grandchildren and the present great grandchildren of whitemen to judge. From that I judge with the present question of the country, none can attempt to do such a fally ⟨folly? cf. p. 86⟩ idea [as] to attack a lion with a maize stalk, and afterwards mauled and battered by the lion, and at last reach his fatal death even to his destruction. Only John won such heroic.

I have far explained about John's Deportments, Patriotism, and Heroic. Now I want to bring out his invisible meaning by doing all these things. By mobilising troops against whitemen, he did not mean that he could defeat him. No. It was only caution, because his first letter was not attended to in which he requested something about his country men. He thought his words in writing were too high, and was not used as if it was a voice from a human being. So he thought to give a caution by striking a blow with a maize stalk and that to give head ⟨heed?⟩ to the whitemen to change the bad treatment towards his country men and women to the betterment.

He did as the old story say, that in a place, somewhere in the North, a lot of monkeys found plenty of fruits food and they were enjoying and living upon that food. One day a huge elephant came over to that forest, where, after entering into the fruit forest, instead of eating the fruits with monkeys, the elephant began to knock and cut down the fruit trees and chewed even the roots of the trees. This kind of action, the elephant repeated often times. The trees were finishing falling. One day the elephant was again doing the same thing. One of the monkeys approached the elephant personally, and ask him to stop felling down the fruit trees, as they, the monkeys, had no other food to live upon—and told the elephant the better way was for him to eat the fruit of the trees in the same way they were eating, by plucking off the fruits only, and have the trees to yield more fruits for next year, and so forth. The elephant paid not a slightest attention to that, now he made a worse of felling the trees he was doing. Monkeys being a small kind of animals, never went on with the matter, although the matter was a grave one, but through fear, he went away.

Next day the monkey came again and sat on one of the fruit trees in the forest, just by the side of the elephant road. The elephant again came passing the same road, a poor monkey then gave a deadly slap on the elephant tail, that slap made the elephant look behind and saw that the slap had been inflicted on his tail by a tiny monkey. He caught him, and asked him, what he meant by it. Monkey replied, I did not mean anything Sir. [The elephant asked:] Why and what made you to slap me? I am too tiny and weak, [the monkey said,] to go on discussing with you and I thought it the best, to give you a signal of my poor slap, that you may understand that the action of felling fruit trees do us a great harm; and I choose to die by being tramped by you, than to die with hunger. The elephant said, you are a fool, poor little monkey, you knew you have no strength to fight me, so as you have made up a fool of yourself, by touching me with your tiny hand. I will now crush you into powder. The monkey was then crushed and finished.

Next day the elephant passed that road again, and when he arrived near that tree, where that monkey was, remembered that slap which he received from a tiny monkey, and for what the tiny animal bravely slapped him, and when he saw the rest of monkeys about eating the fruits from the trees, he thought, if I will fell more fruit trees, surely, these tiny monkeys will look at me as a bad man, though they have no words to speak or power to fight with me. So the elephant at last became ⟨took⟩ pity on the little animals and never fell more fruit trees, but he kept eating in the way the small animals were eating. At the end, the elephant became a big friend and a protector of the small animals. Now do you think that the monkey which was killed by the elephant, with his slap, though with force, meant to kill the huge elephant? If that is your meaning, and thought, you are absolutely wrong. In the same way John meant, I am sure, [his own blow.] I think that has given out a clear explanation of his invisible intention for striking that blow, on a whiteman's tail.

Again I must remind you, that John was one of Kalonga's descendants. I said, that Kalonga was a cunning fellow to lead others for exploring lands, by which he owned the greatness over his own people.

Secondly that Kalonga was cutting the heads of dead people and pack them in baskets, and bringing them to his village from which he owned the name of Kalonga with the interpretation of "Packer."

Now I want to take John for these two accounts. John was also cunning as that of his ancestor Kalonga. He also took up a leading party. Kalonga led people to explore the lands, which ⟨while?⟩ John led people into a conflict, a bloodshed and to the destruction. Secondly, John instructed his troops to cut a couple of heads of white planters who were to be in their hands and bring over to his headquarters for him to see. This is the very way of Kalonga's deeds; with the deads, cutting heads, was he not a peculiar man? Yes, he was.

Now I must look at John for his actions and deeds done, and then compare him to be clearly Kalonga, and that he must be of his own (Kalonga's) family. Surely he must have had a drop of Kalonga's blood in his veins. Does not matter much, how many years past, after Kalonga, the leader of other people. The packer had died, and if none of his other great grandchildren followed his actions and deeds that is ⟨?⟩ John was then supplied with sufficient blood of Kalonga, the conquerer. Therefore, I do not blame him that, why he was born out of Kalonga's family, for which cause, he was innocent. He did not ask he wanted to be born out of Kalonga's family, but he was accidentally born, out of which he did not help himself. He did not ask that he wanted to be born with sufficient drops of Kalonga's blood at all. For an example a ruffian Nguru man, marries Yao woman, who is very lazy, make a son born to them, what you expect that child to be? If he has been supplied with blood from the father, certainly he will be a ruffian. If not to take all the savageness from his father, half or a quarter of it he has it, and will act accordingly. So to blame him means to blame him from being born by that ruffian Nguru which is not cause of his own, and also which he did not help or to know who was causing him. The heredity and atavism are brought into a person created, by the supply of blood from the ancestors, does not matter how many thousands of years after, someone must receive a supply in drops or by certain amount, or quantity of it. He will then act with it accordingly.

Therefore, John's action and deeds were from the heredity and atavism which could not be prevailed [over] by the environment. All wise people understand that environments cannot prevail heredity or atavism. Heredity or atavism is the only thing to control a person in the first place. The environments are his additional but they cannot prevail [over] the control of the two. I cannot go on with it, [but from] what I have stated, I think it is clearly enough with regard to John's action and deeds.

Now I want to know, what name this man may be given? His real name is John Chilembwe. May I call him a Mr. John Brown of America? Why? You are right to say why. I will say briefly, about a Mr. John Brown of America. Many people have read about this man who fought against his Government, it is some years back. Why he did it? He was against slave trading, which was at that time common market to sell and buy Negroes. That trade went on so far, that Mr. John Brown thought to put an end to it. He tried to interview the authorities in person and in writing, none took notice of his words. He then formed up a small army together with his own sons, and fought against his Government. He was defeated, and his army crushed to powder. He himself was compared ⟨judged?⟩, and afterwards executed. That was the end of his army, and himself.[6]

Now after many years, what became to his name? His name has won a great fame. Up to this time, all the military troops march on with a song of Mr. John Brown actions and deeds, although his actions and deeds were seen as criminal offences. Many years after, wise people examined them, and found that they were worth while. So they published them out, and made it known to everyone, and after all they formed a song out of his actions and deeds. The song is still living now, which ⟨although⟩ Mr. John Brown was buried years and years ago.[7]

Can I compare John Chilembwe to be a Mr. John Brown? I know one will question me: who was dealing with slave trading in the time of John Chilembwe, that you should compare him with Mr. John Brown? No. No persons were being sold, but the Laws and Regulations of the country were being sold and bought for ⟨with⟩ respect of colour. I will explain this fully later on. Has the country after John Chilembwe [was] killed and buried won anything which will show to have been won through John Chilembwe? Yes, the country has won the betterment. I will explain this also later, and how the country is enjoying the fruits,

6. It is not known how Mwase knew so much about John Brown.
7. Neither the famous song about John Brown, Charles Sprague Hall's "Glory Hallelujah! Or John Brown's Body"—to which Mwase presumably refers—nor the verses about him by John Greenleaf Whittier ("Brown or Ossawatomie"), Edna Dean Proctor ("John Brown"), and Louise Imogen Guiney ("John Brown: A Paradox") could have provided the information about Brown that is retailed herein by Mwase.

79

which John Chilembwe has laboured. May I compare him with a Mr. William Prynne of England, who in spite of repeated warnings and heavy punishments by imposing heavy fines and sometime by putting him through a pillory, won the freedom of press? [8] Or may I compare him at a Sir Roger Casement of Ireland, who secretly arranged with the Germans to rebel against his own Government? [9] I know the wise men will find which name John Chilembwe may be called after all. I do not know what was Chilembwe's idea, when mobilising troops against his Government. He may perhaps thought to fight the whitemen and become a conqueror himself, as Kalonga his ancestor did, or [he may have] merely [fought] for the Amor Patria; I cannot state which. Because I did not see him personally.

8. William Prynne, a Puritan pamphleteer and enemy of the English Established Church, in 1632 suffered the agonies of the pillory and imprisonment, was fined, and deprived of his Oxford degree after a fanatical exposé of the sinful unlawfulness of stage plays that was interpreted as a personal attack upon the reigning monarch. For libeling the Bishop of Norwich, Prynne was again pilloried and also branded in 1637. Although he was vindicated and released from imprisonment by the Long Parliament in 1641, Prynne later turned against the Commonwealth and was again imprisoned for three years.

9. Casement, after a distinguished British consular and diplomatic career (he received a knighthood in 1911 for his exposés of atrocities by the Peruvian Amazon Company), joined the Irish National Volunteers and, in 1916, landed from a German submarine at the Irish port of Tralee. He was executed for treason.

I am sure I have gone with John Chilembwe's affairs far beyond enough. I cannot say whether wrongly or rightly—that I have left it with the readers to judge. I said, that I will explain later about the buying and selling of Laws and Regulations for [with] respect of colour. I am very sorry I have no wise head to expand this properly, yet, I left it with the wise men to add or to alter the words I have wrongly put in. I say, those days, the Government was indeed very loose to ⟨easy with⟩ the whitemen and strict to the Blackmen of the country. An European Planter would create a law of his Estate, for a native to observe, and if a native does not obey it, he is to be sent to the Boma, where the native was to be punished for that. The whiteman was not to appear in Court at all, but only by his letter. A native was to be punished by the letter's evidence, which evidence, he could not cross-examine it. The whiteman could write to the Boma saying "this native has disobeyed my lawful orders," which orders nobody knew it, and continued, "he must be punished as to set an example for others." This letter was to be accepted as evidence against a native, and there he gets his punishment, that clearly showed that whiteman had to buy the law with the respect of his colour, and that the law was to be sold to him in respect of the colour. Therefore a native, being of a Black colour, could not buy one.[1]

In those days, if a native had complaint against a whiteman, the whiteman was not to be called up to answer the charge, or the suit against him in Court, but only a letter was written to him,[2] and whatever he will reply, that was to be relied upon, and the native was to be judged upon that reply. Often times natives complained of being beaten by whiteman to the Boma ⟨i.e., *complained* to the Boma⟩ but all without satisfactory results. The only conclusion received was that whiteman cannot beat you without offending him ⟨without your having offended him⟩. I know you have offended him; "Choka" ⟨scram!⟩. In those days a whiteman could administer whipping and flogging at his house, or Estate, [and] the Government never interfered or warn him of his actions. I cannot say whether this was out of their view or hearing. For this reason a native feared the whiteman as he fears the polegoblins ⟨?⟩ of heaven. Surely he did not believe there will be a sign of [better] relationship in the future. Often times, [Africans] feared when their master a whiteman has given them a letter to the Boma, if that letter, after addressing it, it had a straight line like this ⸺ at the bottom of the envelope. If they were two they talked to each other, "see, the whiteman has put 'Chikoti' (a whip)

1. African defendants were often denied the opportunity of facing their accusers in minor cases. The white plaintiff usually sent a letter containing his charges to a local magistrate (the district commissioner); when the defendant was summoned to the *boma,* he had to argue against the "letter." The practice naturally occasioned great resentment. Mwase is not implying corruption; he writes only of differential treatment, despite the use of emotive financial words.

2. By the British district commissioner or resident magistrate.

on this letter, so we are going to be flogged." Some other times, they did not deliver such letters, they were to throw or torn [it] even to burn it on a fire. That was through fear of being beaten at the Boma or by any whiteman where that letter was to go. Why they did this? Because they saw a lot of their men being beaten just after the letter was delivered to the Boma or to the whiteman concerned. This I call it Laws trading of the past time.[3]

Native, sometimes, was to work about two to three months without paying him ⟨being paid⟩. When complaining why they should not be paid, the whiteman said "Choka, ngati ufuna ku Boma pita" (bearing the interpretation as go away, if you want to go to the Boma go); and if the native will insist on that, he is to be beaten severely, and afterwards send him to Boma with a letter, in which he ⟨the planter⟩ has had to write that this boy gave me insolence, and such like. There also he would write anything which has made that whiteman not to pay the native, which the whiteman had thought to be important, and for which the Boma would think serious against the native. As the system was to rely on a letter, the native then had to lose his two or three months' pay.

[There were] Many other things, which looked favourable to a whiteman and contrary to the native. This was Law market, as that slave market. The think ⟨I thank⟩ the Blue skies, that such Law market is dispensed. I hope will not be seen again.

I have again asked, if the country has won something extraordinary since then? Yes, the country is far enjoying its quarter betterments tho' not half yet [has been achieved.] Of course, the child born you can-

3. Precise meaning unclear.

not expect it to walk and run by the very [first] week or month. It grows gradually, until it will reach its height. The country has indeed won the best Government, best measures of ruling and even won the Government of no respect of colour. No letter is now used as evidence against a native, does not matter what value is the person who has written if anyone is to lose the case through lack of evidence. "Chapeau bas" system is entirely diminished and vanished.[4] No native fear the town when he has his hat on, [although] this was a very big offence in the days of Chilembwe. Native were often and often beaten for this respect, their complaints were not listened to. This grew worse indeed. The native knew not what to do, in a way of defending his head from the heat of the sun, when passing the whiteman's town.

Now a whiteman is a friend of a native all round, does not matter much about eating etc.[5] Now natives are holding responsible of some work, which were [previously] for only whitemen and others of light colours.[6] The voice of a native is now under consideration, and not to put it aside as [in] past time, although not every word asked, but gradually this will apply. And the Boma officials pay much attentions to what a native say or complains, and then reply him or her satisfactorily, in the same way one could reply to his children. The Boma does not send Askari to catch and tie women in the villages, for the way of collecting taxes from them, nor sending Askari for

4. Raising one's hat to the master, or the white man.
5. That is, it did not matter much to Mwase that whites and Africans could not eat or socialize together.
6. Yet in the 1930's, Nyasa Africans could not advance beyond clerical positions in the civil service or in business. See Rotberg, *Nationalism*, 121–124.

seizing men for the Boma work, as was the system in those days. The Boma has brought into the country a long required official, the Director of Education, whose duty is to encourage the better and higher education to the natives, [and it] does not matter at present, [that] some of the Mission Schools are still weak, they will soon fall into the line. The Government has again encouraged the natives to grow saleable crop, such as tobacco ⟨sun-dried Turkish-type tobacco⟩ and cotton, and provided Inspectors for the work. They have opened up big roads for anybody to pass either by foot or by any kind of vehicles, without hindrance. They have made very expensive bridges in the country for anybody to cross on them without paying anything. They still encourage natives to build brick houses for themselves in their villages. They encourage natives to be agriculturists and some kind of business men in their own country. They have put up a Law, that no land is to be alienated to Europeans or Indians unless that land is not required then by the natives themselves. They have added to the staff a Detachment of Civil Police whose duty is to protect lives and property of both white and black. Cases are properly attended to, with no prejudice or bias to either side. Taxes are properly collected, of course, [those] who evade it should be punished severely. They all know well now, what lovely improvements this money do in the country. Now white and black meet in the streets as friends, and not as enemies as [in] past time. They salute each other in the ordinary way, as one salutes a relative or a country man or woman. Things have come to a great change since then. I am sure to say that we have arrived at the season of better governing. Yes, we are well governed now, far different with that Government in the days of John Chilembwe, which Government is dead and buried along with John and all who were with him.

I am sure, if John Chilembwe was born now and enjoy this newly born Government, certainly, he would have not mobilised troops against it. Does not matter whether he would have been one of very bad feeling, he should have not done so. No person, [even] if perhaps John himself would [have] thought such, could agree with his folly idea. I thank the Heavens, that the old Government with the old Nyasaland is indeed dead and buried, [and that a] newly born Government and Nyasaland is placed instead of the two dead ones.

I believe I have explained all what made old Government and Nyasaland bad, and the goodness of newly born Government and Nyasaland as well. Do not expect one to write everything correct, "Memorabilia" are that a person is born to err etc. I do not mean that things written in my book are all correct. I know that in many points you will agree with me tho' in some points, I am wrong. Therefore instead of blaming me, you should pity me, and instead of hating me, you should help me. Kindly do not feel inconvenient when reading my book for the words wrongly set in. I did not mean to make you feel [that way] about it, and [if] that [happened], put it as the pen's error and the ⟨my⟩ short mental. I wished, I could have wide mental so that I could bring the matter quite clear enough to the minds of people who were to read my book. So I am afraid that instead of explaining things for people to understand I have [obscured things]. Also I know that I have left a lot to be written in which were of most important to the readers, this omission is through defective of memory, and nothing else.

Now I want to touch slightly to the present white Planters. In my opinion the white Planters we have now in the country are not bad Planters as those were in the old Government and country. Those Planters are also dead together with the old Government and country, we have got newly born Planters placed in. They all depend upon what Law the Government has put in for their benefit, and for the goodness of the country also. They do not trouble people. They do not administer flogging at their Estates or houses. In spite of all, it is well understood now by the white Planters and other business men that, by practising cruelty towards their labour, they will lose them, and it is always difficult for such a Planter or a business man to find or keep permanent labour at his work. The native tenants on the Private Estates are given full notices, when to quit the Estate. It is of course his or her own fault, if not to comply with the notice, which is, some time, long enough to enable him or her to prepare the leaving of the Estate. I am ⟨In⟩ some ways, it is not fair to settle on the Private Estates if Crown Land is available in the near vicinity. But as it is always the custom of the country, not to break off villages which have very long standing, unless on a very important reason.[7] I cannot go on much about the white Planters, my conclusion on them is that they are all good men, and [he] who is a bad Planter knows himself or herself for not obtaining regular labour on his work. That does not make the country men feel at all, but it harms the Planters himself or herself.

7. These conclusions were denied by the contemporary African political associations of which Mwase was a member and a sometime official. See Rotberg, *Nationalism*, 33–36, 119–120.

● AUTHORS INCONSISTENT WITH REGARD THE FRIENDSHIP BETWEEN ASIATICS AND NATIVES

Would I be allowed to go on, and put down certain notes regard the Indian, a person from Asia who followed whitemen or who came up [to Nyasaland] with no other purpose, but to earn money on the country, either by business or by the work.[1] Why I want to write few notes about this person, is about the general talk in the country that they are bad people, their intention is to root up and even blot off all the drops of gold, silver and copper for their home, in India. Is it not so? Yes, it is clearly so. This talk is among the whitemen and the natives of the country. Why they think this? Is this correct? Now I stand oppose it. I oppose it strongly. Thoughts of this kind is indeed wrong. I would also advise my fellow native, not to say it again, if had said it before. Why I stop him? I clearly say that the only close friend of a native, the Asiatic business man is the only man in the country, who feels sympathy on a native man and woman. He helps a native far beyond that help a native can receive from the European business man. A native can bother an Indian as much as he could, asking him to give him some clothes or

1. By 1931, about 6,000 Indians lived in Nyasaland, primarily in the Shire Highlands area. Their number included Sikhs, Gujerati-speaking Banians *(bannia)*, and Punjabis. "By the work" probably means "by working for the Government."

88

anything in his store for credit. An Indian, who look to a native with much sympathy and ready to help when in need, is then forced by his kind heart to give him.

Why should a native blame on Indian for taking away gold, silver and copper to his home in India? Where could he keep his thrives? An Indian man is a thriver as well as a European. Both these men are in a great contest of gaining the profit in the country and send it to their homes. Obviously speaking, they are both carrying away the gold, silver and the copper off the country for theirs ⟨to their own country⟩. Why then to blame one and agree with another while the two are guilty of one offence? Generally speaking, the people say that the European Traders spent all their profit money in the country, while the Indian Traders do not. How does they know this? Who can explain me the discrepancy on these two Traders? They accuse an Indian [of] clothing ⟨collecting?⟩ off the dew on the meadow, and recommend the other as flourishing the dry meadow. How? I stand oppose it. Why? Yes, I will say it, does not matter wrongly or rightly, let me oppose it. Before I start to say anything about it, I ask you to listen me gently, and then watch my explanation on the matter.

First I want to take an Indian Trader, who is accused of blotting off the country of her riches. This man came on and opened a trading store in the middle of natives and [whether he] deal business with them fairly or unfairly that depends upon himself. There he prosper gradually, and afterwards he become a rich man at home and here. He sends away what he can lay hold on, and keep in the country what can help him to carry on with. What he sends

out is what [he needs] to meet his dues ⟨?⟩ and that
for his family[2] and parents to live on with, and the
rest of that is for safety for his future use. That remains here is that for drawing more profit, and for
living upon himself, and the rest for paying his Rents,
Licences, his casual labour. He pays Licences and
Rents to the Government in the same way a European
Trader do. He employs labour and pay them as European Trader do. Where is the difference then? The
difference I see to that of a European is the kind
heart of an Indian Trader towards a native. In spite
of credit trade with natives ordinance ⟨the ordinance
relating to credit trade with natives⟩, he is ready to
reply ⟨i.e., help⟩ the native by supporting him of his
needs, which encourages the native to come into a business life. While the European Trader thinks to support
the native in the way an Indian Trader do was to lose,
but to stick to the credit trade with natives ordinance
was the way to safety.[3]

An Indian Trader remembers that, when I ⟨the trader⟩
left home for Africa for the purpose of business, I
meant to carry business in Africa with the Africans,
and not with Europeans, for he could not trouble
himself coming to Africa and open a store when he
wanted to deal with Europeans, it was then for him
to open his store in Europe. And if his intention was
to deal business with his Indian fellows, his store
would have been opened in India, somewhere in Bom-

2. His extended, not his nuclear, family.

3. The regulation referred to was a governmental ordinance that
prohibited traders from extending credit to Africans in an usurious
fashion. By so doing it prohibited installment buying. It was intended to protect Africans, but Mwase seems to argue throughout
this and the next two paragraphs that Asians should be praised
for disregarding the provisions of the ordinance.

bay, Calcutta, Janinager Dendad ⟨Jamnagar?⟩, Kathi-
awar or Lalpur ⟨Kolhapur?⟩. So I call an Indian Trader
the dearest friend of a native of this country, a man
ready to fall in for a help to the native. He is brave
to stand in favour of a native in spite of many warnings towards ⟨against⟩ helping a native. A native of
this country is relying on an Indian Trader. The Indian also rely on a native as his close friend and a
customer. This clears an Indian Trader out of being
accused of robbing or blotting off the riches of the
country. He is as good as the other and as bad as
the one, in respect of this accusation.[4]

Now turn and look the European Trader. Yes, he has
best and durable stuff in his trading store for a native
to be attracted on them. He deals no "Kunyenga"
⟨misrepresentation⟩ in his dealings, but he is too rigid.
He has no defective memory towards the regulation
relating to credit trade with natives. He is [not] afraid
of a native on cash term basis. But when a native
is empty handed or impecunious, he does not look at
him or to listen to his complaints towards a help
on loan or credit. He is good to give the native on
cash basis the real price of his goods without swin-
dling in prices. But too rigid. He cannot bend to the
help of a native, does not matter on what arrangement a native may try to make with him. He thinks
a great loss may soon occur on dealing with a native
according to the regulation relating to the credit trade
with natives. Yet, he loses tremendously with the people he thinks they are out of that regulation, and

4. The other? And the one? Presumably, Mwase means that
the Indian was no worse or better than the European in this
respect.

who he think they are better and worth while than a native is.[5]

Beside that what I have said about an Indian Trader, his valueness in this country is that he does not put two doors for two different kind of colours. A native when he enters an Indian Trading store, he enters by any door. The Indian himself has fixed up doors of entrance for everybody, not as a European Trader who fixes up two doors for each colour, and if a native has entered through a door which is for the Europeans he has offended the European Trader, who is to drive the native by the words of "Choka," Pita khomo wina, uyu khomo wazungu!! (This bears interpretation of go away, come in by the other door, this door is for the European.) There, the native is, indeed, caught with much shame of his colour, and he blames the creator, why he created him of that colour which has no respect or value on the face of the world. Sometimes he returns back without going in, does not matter he wanted that kind of goods to buy, he has to vanish up his mind for such a particular goods, and then change his mind to go to an Indian Trader and buy, does not matter different to the goods he wanted, he thinks it is far better to be comforted by the Trader tho' the goods may look somewhat [shoddier], than to buy the better goods wanted, and receive shame from the Trader before you buys the goods.[6]

5. I.e., Europeans and Asians.
6. In colonial Nyasaland, Northern Rhodesia, and Southern Rhodesia, European-owned establishments and many governmental facilities set aside a special entrance for Africans. Often Africans were not even allowed inside the stores but were instead served through a hatch in one wall. Europeans frequently refused to allow Africans to handle beforehand the goods that they intended to buy. These practices generally continued until the 1950's.

And oft-times the educated natives of nowadays, they do not go to such a store or an office which has respect of colours ⟨color discrimination⟩ knowing that they bear inferior colour to that of the other fellows. They are ashamed to be shown a door or a window which is to meet their colours by entering or standing through that, while the other door is unoccupied, but simply because his colour does not suit an entrance by that door. Is this not absurd to a European Trader to raise such segregation? The money the native has is the same coin, bearing same King ⟨George V⟩ and value, but he is despised for bearing inferior colour on his body, which is not his own fault, but the creator.

For the forebeared reason, an Indian Trader is very much valued by a native of this country, so if the system of European Trader will remain as it is now, certainly an Indian Trader will be of much value in the future even. Therefore it will be a very big mistake for a native to join the column of accusing an Indian Trader to be the "blot off man" but to take him as his dear friend and who is ready to fall in for a help.

I am sure my native fellows will agree to my observation in regard the two Traders in the country. I am glad both these men are spending their money, which they pay to the Government, and which money the Government is spending it in developing our country by opening more useful roads, bridges and valuable buildings, which make the country look beautiful. I am also glad that both men are helping the improvement of our country by opening such business and estates and when they employ our men and pay them accordingly.

I have observed this in the way of clearing out some bad feelings among the Indian Traders of the country who were so anxious with the word "blot off man." About half a dozen of the Indian Traders murmured on this, does not matter they did not feel it much, but as a matter of fact, things start little by talk and it grows bigger afterwards. So I am afraid in case our grandchildren will fall in the same mistake again if there is nothing to show them clearly how things stand. I know some will stand obstinate to my observations.

● "FELINS NULLINS": WHO HOLDS RESPONSIBILITY FOR A MULATTO? [1]

The above question is very important, and requires answer or an explanation. A Mulatto is a child born by a whiteman out of a black woman or African woman, who is now roughly called a half-caste. This person has a lot of his comrades in the country. I want to know who is responsible of this person in the country? Why I put this question is because I see him or her stand by himself or herself. No one agrees with him or her. This person stands at the adjoining of two roads, one of which is leading towards his or her father and another go towards the mother. This person stands at that adjoining of the two roads and lingering about there. For him to take the road leading to his or her father is too shining and to proceed by it, he or she meets with rays which shoot straight his eyes and make him not to go any further by that road. He or she turns on to the road which leads to mothers, he or she see that the road is too murky and cannot permit him or her to go on by that road. Otherwise he will or she will face into a pit suddenly, for the road is covered with heavy dark. After all this, person stands gigging about and not knowing where to lean to. He is looked with a disdainful countenance by his father, he is called

1. "Felins Nullins" probably should be *filius nullius,* nobody's children.

a bastard by his own father. Yea, even comparing him to be a hyena's descendant. The mother side rejects him and compares him a Spectre or Phantom from unknown skies. There, he is left by himself hobbling behind.[2]

Now, who is this person? He belongs to which of the three generations? Is he one of Noah's generation? Is he one of Noah's generation?[3] If so, Noah's generation is divided into three only. From that epoch there has not been a fourth generation introduced in the world, no, none, as we all know that the first generation from Adam was only one, [and in the] third generation from Noah there are only three generations. This has been so up to this present Era, in which time we are in third generation of the world.

Now then let us look and intimate the reason why this man is left out and why he is rejected by his mother even. On the first place I must blame the whiteman, who was attracted by a black woman and had intercourse with her, knowingly that the intercourse may cause to bring out something figured as a human being, of which he was responsible to look after as his child. He, the whiteman, after causing a child out of a black woman, remembers that he was a whiteman, a man of superior colour, and that he had made a mistake to intercourse with a black woman and caused a child by her. He then made up his motions ⟨emotions⟩ by chasing away the black woman from him and told her to take away her child with

2. In 1931, the population of Nyasaland included about 1,000 known coloureds, mixed bloods, or mulattos. All three names were used, the first predominantly. The several Nyasaland native associations frequently discussed and sought the alleviation of this problem. They unavailingly urged the Government to make intercourse between white men and African women illegal.

3. The duplication of this sentence very likely is a typing error.

her to her home and come not more. There the woman with her inferior colour and her light coloured child go looking behind with a confide ⟨with confidence⟩ that the whiteman will give hand in looking after this child, which has been caused by him, and who has a lighter [colour] than she. All hope in vain, the poor woman looks after the child herself. The whiteman care nothing of the child caused by him. He does not say even to his comrades that he is a parent of a child.[4]

What care of a child the poor woman will do? The woman feeds the child with insufficient food and supplies insufficient cloths. She does not know what drugs or medicines to give the child when sick. She is sometimes afraid to take the child to the European hospital in case the European physician is going to ask by whom she received such light coloured child. And sometimes she is ashamed before other people that they are to think that she was a bad woman, who go about in the towns with intentions of having intercourses with whitemen.

Now the child grows differently either weak or useless. This has caused a decrease in knowledge, health and wealth among the Mulattos. There are very few people of this race who are well up while the rest is the group of fantastical fools.

Who is the responsible of this fault? Why, certainly is the fault of the causer. Who is the responsible causer in this respect? Father has all the responsibility of the child caused. The person to entice another is always the man, in few cases is the woman. Why then a whiteman hates this woman and even abhor the child caused by him? Was it not better for him

4. This was the usual, but not the universal, response.

to tend this edification before the allurement? What is the badness [that] is in a child after caused and born? He has received light colour than that of mother, that means he has received amount of ⟨more⟩ drops of father's blood in him than that of mother. Why he is not taken in as a proper child of the white-man? Surely the whiteman is the leading parent of this child [with a greater] share than the share the mother has in it.

Now look what kind of a mistake this child make after being brought up by mother only, that means no proper instructions he received from the poor woman, who is not intelligent in this respect, leave the child grow without proper instructions how to carry on with the people and world. The child after all dislike the mother, even the relatives of his mother, because they are bearing dark colours on their bodies when he is light, and often times disagreement is raised between [them] which leads into antagonism. I do not blame him for this mistake because he had no father all his life to instruct him the right word to speak to the people or to his mother or her rela-tives. So what he does is that which he thinks himself to be right which in the eyes of others is looked upon as bad. I do not blame him for not welcoming the father in the way one could do, because he tried that at the beginning but was replied with very bad result from his father, who instead of receiving the welcome from him as a son, he looked at him with contemptuous, even frightened him.

I do not blame the whiteman for chasing away the woman at all, this is quite common practice to every man of any colour to chase a woman under any cir-cumstances which arises, but the chasing of a woman does not apply to a child. Also, of course, the living or intercourse between the whiteman and the black woman is a temporary one. I do not say that it is a marriage, that makes him to take away entirely the children from the woman. Please bear this [in] mind, that it has only the intercourse which is a temporary. Can you call the offspring also temporary one? How? You mean to say that why ⟨they⟩ were born with temporary colours which will change to permanent colours afterwards? To what colour? No, the colour he has received from his father is permanent one and will not change to another. Therefore he should be taken in as a permanent son of a whiteman although may be regarded as a illegitimate child by others, but should be looked after by father.

This case now stands as this: The whiteman refuses that the Mulatto child is not a whiteman ⟨denies that the mulatto child is a whiteman⟩. If I say he is, he says he is not. [If] I look to the Mulatto child and say you are a native, he says I am not a native. So the case stands open without connecting it. Why the Mulatto child refuses to be a native? Yes, he is right, this fault is not his, [it] is that of his father who first refused him to be a whiteman. He also refuses to be a native. Who is to be blamed among these two? The father must be blamed on the first place. If the father would take him as his own son even tho' spurious child and look after him properly, surely he ⟨the mulatto⟩ could also do the likewise with his mother and the mother's relatives; he could do all what he could to ⟨should for?⟩ his mother, even to the mother's relatives. So he is controlled by the heredity and atavism of his father, whose hereditary habit is to desert his own children. Through the drops of that blood from father, he is also deserting his mother and all mother's relations. Why should you blame him for that? He is not a .... of his own ⟨cause of his own misfortune?⟩.

This child should be taken in by the father as his own son, does not matter much in which way of the two ⟨?⟩, there is no reason why this child should not be brought up by the father in the presence of any whitemen's assembly. What hinders him to be a sharetaker of his father's property? Certainly he has right blood of that whiteman and also of his mother as well. I do not know if I am wrong on this point of view in regard the above question and the reply thereto. I trust it is clearly enough for people to agree with me, or not.

● OUTWARD AND INWARD OF THE PRISON AND PRISONERS

My remarks on the above prison and prisoners subject will clear out a bad and evil feeling among natives who regard the prison to be the more cruel practice of the whitemen in the country.[1] The general feeling of the natives outwardly towards prison, especially Central Prison of the Protectorate [in Zomba], is very clumsy. When their relatives are sentenced and sent to Central Prison from their respective districts, the remaining relatives hold up sermony ⟨ceremony?⟩ of lamentation and lost their confidence of seeing him again back from that prison. They believe that when a person is taken away from his district to Central Prison, the only way the whitemen do with such a person, is to batter, to scourge, to buffet, they lance him his flesh with knives or something like it, stone him with stones, prick him with thorns or such like, or even to burn him to death. They again think that the whitemen at that prison do not pay attention to the prisoner's complaint, does not matter he complains of being ill, they do not support him with medicines which would help his recovery, the medicine they give is that to finish his life. They do not give him food to eat sometime a week or so. They give him work of a month to finish it in an hour,

1. Mwase had already served almost a year in prison for theft by a servant of the state.

which, after finishing it he will be taken to a serious illness and possibly die with it. And no physicians are to look after the sick prisoner. If a physician appears there, his duty is to give out medicines which will cause the prisoner die quickly.

They ⟨the relatives of prisoners⟩ think also that when he is taken there [he] is not allowed to open his mouth and to talk to anyone there during all his time he will be there. They think he is not allowed even to drink enough water which would allay his thirst, nor to allow him to wash his body properly. They also think that the prisoner at that prison is not even allowed to sleep without first flog or whip him. They think that he is allowed to look at a certain place during the time, and if he turns and look another place he is severely battered to death. They think the whitemen are truculent people to a prisoner. They are almost ⟨more?⟩ grieved on their relative when he is told he is to be sent to Central Prison, than the relative who is dead and carrying him to grave. They think that the dead person will find to great "Chauta" (Great god), and that he is at rest. But to one sent to prison, especially to Central Prison, they grieved more for him. They say it is an awkward place, clumsy and an ungraceful place is the Central Prison.

Why they feel so ill like this? Yes, I know why it is so. Before the whitemen came in this country, there was no prison or prisoner. We cannot translate in our languages the names prison and prisoner. Prison we translate it as "Nyumba ya Akaidi" ⟨house of prisoners⟩. Prisoner bear a translation of "Kaidi." The translation "Kaidi" had no existence in this country's tongues, but it came over by the slave traders, from far north. In this country there has been no prison houses or prisoner although captives were existed.

The captivity of those days in this country was quite different one in comparison with the whitemen's prison and prisoner. Captives in our tongue we called "Mikoli." These Mikoli are translated to captives in English but the meaning is slightly different. The Mikoli in our old days did not mean only people captured at the war and taken home as war prisoners, and treat them as enemies. Mikoli meant anybody kidnapped and hold back for a ransom, or captured for the debt which another person had owed, and which is still due unpaid.[2] He then had to lie await somewhere near that village where his debtor was used to be, does not matter a relative or not. After capturing such a person he used to call out to the people in that village where the captive lived, telling them in a call that they must not wonder, if a person is missed at their village, and that they should follow him at his village. He used to shout and his name village and the cause of his seizing that person. Secondly, [Mikoli] meant a person seized due to the delay of fixing up a particular case, which case never implicated the person captured by. So Mikoli meant innocent people captured for the offences committed by others, does not matter relative or not, simply being a villagemate or about so, such people were called Mikoli. If none to ransom him at all, then was to be called a slave and was either to be sold, exchange something else or do the slave work, and treated as a slave, which treatment was very worse at the beginning and excellent at last, if the [captive] proved

2. Forms of debt peonage were more common elsewhere in Africa. See Mary Douglas, "Matriliny and Pawnship in Central Africa," *Africa,* XXXIV (1964), 301–313.

himself satisfactory to his master. I do not like to describe how bad was treatment at the beginning or how excellent was his last treatment, my intention is only to differ the name prisoner with the meaning "Mikoli," and to show that there had been no prison house or prisoner in the name, as it is with the white-men now.

This I believe has fixed up the argument of prisoners and the Mikoli clearly enough. A prisoner means a person under arrest, he cannot go out to wash by himself, he cannot put on a cloth he like to put on except prison uniform. He cannot eat what would suit his requirements but only that laid down by the prison officer. He is cut off entirely from his family or relatives only to see or to talk to them on certain occasions, if any fortune may occur. He is to be shut up early in the afternoon, when his intention was not to go to bed by that time. He is given a limited liberty to read or write something. He is prohibited to take a walk by himself at any time unless a warder is behind him armed. He is given a certain blanket to cover and no other kind he can use. He is cut off from all communications, except that .... ⟨which goes⟩ through the prison officer, and such also must be limited. He is prohibited from smoking if he was such an one, even to snuff any kind of tobacco. He is also stopped to salute anyone passing by, although a well known relative or friends, until his time of imprisonment is expired.

This was not the case with Mikoli in old days. The Mikoli were allowed anything to do without interfering him, only going back to his home was not allowed at first. He was allowed to keep his family with him or marry another woman while in the Mikoli system. There were no particular cloths for Mikoli or any kind of food which was given to a Mikoli to eat. He ate anything his master ate, no limitation of liberty in chatting to people or in communicating to anybody he liked to, no armed person to walk behind him. He could have a walk at any distant or to absent himself from his master's village for some days, weeks or months on a visit where he wanted to go as long [as] he had told his master where he was going to and for how many months he would be away. He could make as much ⟨as much money?⟩ he liked and could drink beer over his limited power, was allowed all kind of enjoyments while under the term of Mikoli. He was working for his master by himself, no armed person to watch his back. Besides those, he was allowed certain privileges, he could practice all slave trade himself also, he could go out hunt human beings, sometimes he could also capture his own Mikoli and hand them over to his master, and many other privileges.

So this clearly differs prisoners to be translated to Mikoli in the languages of this country. This also shows obviously, that there has been no prison or prisoner previous to the arrival of the whitemen in the country. Do you still stand obstinate to my explanation, and you still say we had prisoners in our old days? If there is one, who thinks that "Mikoli" meant prisoners, is quite mistaken. Prisoner means a person committed an offence or a crime, prisoner means an offender or a culprit, even a criminal, not a person for the crime done by another or for the debt of another [who] is to be called a prisoner in the eyes of the whitemen. Therefore, there has been no prisoner in the country before the arrival of the whitemen but there has been Mikoli which slightly differs from the term of prisoner. Therefore, under the above circumstances, the people in this country with the exception of the educated people, do [not] understand what prisoner means. But the old people and some other uneducated people [do not] tho' some are gradually copping the meaning.

The greater number of people still say that, the whitemen to send a person to Central Prison means to use country ⟨cruelty?⟩ on him, and think they use any amount of barbarism to a prisoner sent to Central Prison, which cruelty would cause his rapid death. This has been built in their minds up to this time. Why they think all this? The reason is due to the old brute native Askari who were employed at the first instant, who were more ⟨mere⟩ ruffians, and treated their country people in most treatment ways when they were sent to arrest a culprit at a village, they had to tie and such a person against a tree in the face of his villagers etc. and began to beat him to death, sometimes strip off the cloth from him and called his mother or mother-in-law to sit by him, when he is so tied against the tree naked, and many other brutality. Sometimes they could do more than that to a person when he is under arrest. By that, the villagers thought it was instructed by their master, to do all these savageness to people, when they are being arrested at their villages, in the presence of their family mothers or mother-in-laws. This brought them to a conclusion that, the person sentenced, and sent to Central Prison he gets more fatal punishment than that which a native ruffian had done. They thought it was the whitemen's order to that ruffian to harm his own people. This, up to this time, still built in their minds and [they] believe a prisoner is fatally treated by the whitemen in the Central Prison. Of course, it will indeed take a very long time to clear it out of people's thoughts.

For this particular reason, I forced my mind to correct [the beliefs] slightly in this book of mine, by making certain remarks about the prison and the prisoner, and try to make it clear to them, the kindness the whitemen do to a prisoner when sent to Central Prison. Inwardly ⟨from the inside⟩, I witness the graceful, the whitemen do to a prisoner, when admitted in the Central Prison.

I was one of the outwardly news believer ⟨one of those on the outside who believed the whitemen mistreated African prisoners⟩, but when I was found guilty of an offence and sentenced to a couple of years, [I] was sent to Central Prison where to save ⟨serve⟩ the term of my imprisonment. At the arrival there [I] was accompanied by certain fellow convicts. The first thing we were told was [that we were] to be examined by a physician to find out if one of us was attacked by any kind of sickness for which, if found, to be treated first, and no work to be given to him until he is properly healed. This was so, certain of my fellow convicts were admitted into the hospital for treatment for some weeks, without doing any kind of work. The care the patients received in that Central Prison hospital, I have not seen it anywhere else in my life. Mind you, I have travelled greatly and have seen many hospitals in the country and many other countries also, but the treatment done to a prisoner in the Central Prison hospital, I have not seen it anywhere else. I do not say, that other hospitals treat their patients unsatisfactory, no, but I mean to say the way the hospital people do in this particular hospital is indeed different to that which other people do in their hospitals. No other hospital can take such trouble of examining a person who look fit and who does not complain of any pain in his body. This hospital does that, and many prisoners are admitted into hospital without them (the prisoners) to know what pains them, and without feeling anything in his body. What he knows is the only ⟨only the⟩ medicines given him, and afterwards he is being told that he had something wrong in his body, for which they are now treating him. Now, see, who else can match this? Other hospitals system is to wait at the person to come, and complain of pain, on which they are ready to examine him, and then treat him, if anything bad found within him. Well, this is quite common practice to every hospital, therefore the system of this hospital is indeed extraordinary one.

This is one of the greatest things I had watched carefully. Another is about the close attention of the prison officers to their prisoners. They watch carefully upon his health, soon they point out to the Medical Officer if there is something wrong with the prisoner's body or if the prisoner loses his weight. They have given instructions of weighing prisoners every month ending. [If] a prisoner is found losing weight, does not matter whether the prisoner is not complaining any pain, that prisoner is to be admitted into the hospital and receive treatment until something wrong is found out by the physician. He will be kept under physician's treatment, he will be lying there until the Doctor or any of his men satisfy that he is gaining back his weight and that he is well to do the work. These officers watch also on any prisoner [to see] that he gets his food, his cloth, his blanket, his room, and also that he gets his bath for his body, and to see that he receives soap to wash his cloth every Sunday. They are like parents to the children.

Prisoners who are flogged are those who do not obey the prison regulations, and who refuses or fight with the warders, and some [who] are committing petty offences after repeated exhortations. These prisoners, of course, they deserve to be flogged as much [as] they could be flogged to try to stop them committing trifling offences inside the prison. Yet, in many cases when such floggings are inflicted on these convicts a Medical Officer is first to examine him, if fit to be flogged. And on other occasions the Medical Officer is to stand by, when such flogging is being carried on. Well, anybody can punish his children at any time if the children do not obey what the parents order them to do, or order them not to touch. Therefore this is not stranger or does it mean cruelty at all.

The prisoners in the prison, they are indeed happy, than any other prison in the country. On top of their usual food, they are given meat twice every week, rice the same, when it is available in stock. Besides that, they are supplied with sugar-canes, bananas, potatoes, pumpkins, cassava ⟨manioc⟩, even mangos and lemons. The supply of these articles to prisoners means great kind[ness] towards them, there is no other prison officer in this country can do such kind[nesses] to prisoners.

I must suggest that Central Prison of this kind should be pronounced as Prizzon; not prison, as it is now. Its pronunciation should be heavy and bear double z between. Prison sounds too light. This pronunciation prison should be applied to outside prisons, which prisons are at present in the responsibility of native warders only, and where a European officer visits occasionally, and where prisoners are not properly looked after by these native warders. They sometimes beat the prisoners with no proper reason to do so. The Central Prison officers do not allow any warder to take law into his own hand, and beat any of the convicts. If a convict has infringed any prison law, the only way for the native warder to do is to bring such a convict before the prison officer, who is to hold a court, and if found guilty of that, the convict is to be punished by his order to flog him or to give him an extra work in the afternoon, when others go in for their beds, and sometimes the convict loses his marks which he earned. No order [is given] by the prison officer to native warders to beat the prisoners by themselves at any day or time. If one native warder will do that he is liable to some kind of punishments.

The prisoners are laughing, talking and singing. They make such sort of noise to enjoy themselves. They are also allowed to pray on every Sundays, read their books and chatting to each other. The only surprising character I have seen among the convicts is the enticing of a young man, who bears pretty good looking. Certain men begun to entice the young boy or man to come and stay with him at their rooms in the prison. They sometimes quarrel between them or hate each other for the sake of a young boy. I cannot understand the meaning of quarreling for a young boy at all. Not all the convicts who entice the youths but the certain amount of them do so, while the rest wonder to that character. I think to watch it so closely, one can find out why they entice these youths and create quarrel between themselves.

I can strongly recommend the general treatment towards the convict in the Central Prizzon. No Planter can care [for] his labour, such as Prizzon officers care [for] their convicts. It is indeed very wonderful that these convicts are so estimated, very much worth. His Excellency the Governor specially comes to see them and also see their rooms where such dirty and filthy people sleeps and examine even their food and such like in the prison, leaving important work of the country. His Honour the Judge also comes specially to ask the convicts if they have any complaints to make, wasting his valuable time for such evil doers, and many other important Government officials, including the Chief Inspector of Prison. All these important people waste their valuable time on gazing on the convicts, the people who deserved to be burned to ashes or to be thrown in the deep water as payment to their evil doing. When these important people come into the Central Prison, they do not ask any of the warders to lay his complaint to them or anybody else there except only a convict. Do you not agree with me then, that a convict is very much highly estimated before the Government?

Yes, I know you do, no important official can come to your house at your village or anywhere else and ask you to lay a complaint before him. Only a D. C. ⟨district commissioner⟩ on his village travelling can come and speak to you, then you can complain to him of your trouble, but not specially for you at your house or at any other place. Look and see what is done to the convicts, is that not grace? yes, it is most kind towards the malefactors. The Prizzon management is indeed excellent. Death rate is very much less, I can say it is more less than at a village where such number of people as that may be found. The Superintendent of that Prizzon has more influence over his malefactors. A word, he gives it out as an order, all the convicts take it. Mind you, he is not a cruel man, but he likes to see the order issued, done accordingly, by the convicts. If one of the convicts evades it, he will get his punishment either by flogging or his marks or days of his remission he had earned. This regard to the order issued has taught the malefactors to follow the better than to go on with what they thought to go on with it, if there should be a slight relax in his dealings with them.[3] He loves all his convicts and hates all, if they do not obey the lawful orders. There is no maladministration or malediction in dealing with the convicts by the Superintendent or any of the European officers. The only maledictions received by the convicts are those from the native chief warder who abuses anyone without cause. This is done ⟨due?⟩ to his brutality, as he does not understand the different between convict and the slavery. So he uses the word slave, when insulting a convict. He is one of the old type of the Askari whose duties were to wrong and mischief people, which to them was as good as music while to others was does ⟨dose?⟩ melancholy. This is the only genuine complaint of officers' abuses or insult [to] a convict by calling him a slave, only that brute native chief warder.

Another complaint the convicts inwardly lay is about the shaving [their heads] with razor of every Sunday.

3. Sentence unclear. Punctuation, beginning with the word "regard," has been left exactly as in the typescript.

This of course is very danger to their brains as they are working on a very hot sun with clean ⟨bare⟩ heads as those without anything to protect them. This indeed, although the matter may be minimized, does matter, not much, but it has some slight injuries to their heads and minds, unless [they wear] some kind of "Kofia," a cap, made out of a cloth, like the convicts in Dar-es-Salaam, Tanganyika Territory, do. I believe that this will be looked at later on tho' it is now omitted.

There is nothing else of what an inward convict can complain while he is running the term of imprisonment in this Prizzon. Convicts [who] complain of maladministration are those [in] outside prisons which are entirely in full care of the native warders. Those convicts are being beaten and the warder's way of controlling their native convicts is very bad. The case is due that most of these native warders are pure brutes of the old type, whose duties is to spoil the melody of the European regulations, and think to better it with savageness. This will take a very long time for the Europeans to correct the errors of these uncivilised people, and make them to fall in. [It] does not matter [if] he is told properly by the European not to do this or that, but this. He is ready to say yes, but as soon [as] the European who had been instructing him disappears [from] his sight, he does the very thing he was instructed not to do. I agree it is not the European fault indeed. Therefore, I am very much gratefulness (on behalf of my country people) for the kind treatment the country people received when under the term of imprisonment in this Prizzon.

I wonder if divine treatment towards the sinners is like his one which our local Government is doing to its sinners. I think the divine punishment to sinners is more better than the Government man do. Picking out from what I am taught, the divine punishment is very cruel. There is no mercy or grace towards a convict, who is to be convicted by the divine court. I do not know whether I am wrongly taught in this respect. Out of what I am taught is clearly that once you are convicted by the divine court and sentenced to everlasting punishment, [you have] no food, cloth, water, no physician to see you or to attend you. Nobody to listen to your complaints or cries whatsoever. No Angel or anyone from the Royal Palace to come and visit you or to ask you to lay a complaint to him of what ⟨how⟩ you are being treated by the Superintendent Satan or any of his officers of that prison (Hell), and no privileges are given to those convicts under the Superintendent Satan and his officers.

Please do not call me arrogancy, I am only quoting this as an emperiously ⟨?⟩ against the divine court. I mean to say that the Government do all its kindness towards its sinners, who are sent from the court of man to Central Prizzon. I think I have written all about the Prizzon, Prison and the Prisoners as well. If I am wrong please do not call me insane[4] but one thing should be remembered, that "hominisest errar." [5] Therefore do not throw stones on me.

4. Mwase may have known that many European officials thought him "mad" or insane because of his multifarious campaigns and his habitual tendency to launch verbal broadsides against the Government.

5. *Hominis est errare,* man errs.

This country now is full up with the Whiteman's Law, the old country's law is diminished, no one uses the old laws, but the old customs are still standing to life tho' some of them are diminished and torn to pieces. The whiteman's law is very popular. Of course a certain number of the whiteman's law does not need ⟨meet⟩ the natives' satisfaction. I can mention one law which natives of this country do not agree of its decision. Adultery is one which gives a lot of doubts in the way the whiteman decide it. The whiteman's law asks this as civil case which has no much importance. [By] The country's law, this is one of the capital charge or the capital crime which [was] followed with death sentence by consuming the both culprits with fire, or a nobkery ⟨knobkerrie⟩ [or] even a spear would play his flesh or her flesh until they were both perished. Their dead organs were not to be cared for. And sometimes both the culprits were to be given away by cutting parts of their bodies such as ears, arms, nose or something else in the way of emasculation. This was of course very cruel punishment for people to bear.[1] But the whiteman's law is very much relaxed in dealing with this case. I am

1. Ethnological accounts appear to discount Mwase's report of the punishments meted out to adulterers. In most of the Malawi societies, adultery was regarded in a less severe light.

115

afraid such slackness in this respect encourages the crime to be done publicly or without a bit of shame. Among the people of this country this kind of crime is the only cause of a many murders and arsons. Unless the compensation or the sentence is raised to a higher scale than it is now, these two crime will continue to grow big in the country.

Another [problem] is about a young lady or woman, who is not married yet and whom the parents are still looking after with expectation to espouse her to a better man for marriage in the near future.[2] Another whimsical fool wheedles her and falls into adultery with her without the permission of her parents. This is also a case which the whiteman's law say absolutely nothing against it. It is said that both are free agents and can arrange or agree whatsoever is between them. This brings the parents of that young body more afflictions. When a girl is so young—does not matter she is passed her age—but she is too easy to be allowed by a man and consent to what he asks without her understanding the danger of so doing. In this case the man should be blamed and given punishment. It is standing at the same door with another adultery which has been explained before.

Other dealings in this cases are very popular; I think the whiteman's law to prohibit Mwabvi ordeal.[3] I

2. The author presumably refers to the practice of bridewealth, whereby the prospective husband's family traditionally secured the marriage bond with a payment or a series of payments to the bride's family.

3. Originally the special ordeal poison made from the bark of a particular tree (*Erythrophleum guineense*), the term *Mwabvi* later came to mean any kind of ordeal by means of which Africans traditionally determined the guilt or innocence of their fellows. By "I think," Mwase may have meant "I think particularly of." Conceivably he meant "I thank," for "think" appears several times

quite agree with the whiteman that this [ordeal] does very great harm to the lives of people without any [re]course. I entirely deny the witchcraft's affairs. It is indeed a great waste of time to pay attention to it. It is almost foolish to believe that there is witchcraft of any sort. If there is anyone who still believes on it, I call him an idiot. I thank the Heavens this is dispersing among the country people.

I know some of my country people will be against my suggestion in regard the severe punishments to be inflicted in both cases of adultery, because the play ⟨compensatory pay?⟩ is of more profitable to them and of great loss to others. I do not mean that the severe punishment would lessen the crime to be committed, no, but to frighten the offenders to extend it largely as they think to do. This is the only big crime among the people in this country which creates enmity and disagreement between them. With our old laws in this connection they were afraid when they saw others being consumed with the flames of fires to their finish. Therefore this crime was seldomly committed, and once it was discovered they were then to believe they were to be perished by fire.

Another whiteman's law which puzzles the natives in this country is the prohibition of cutting trees and shooting or killing game and game birds.[4] No person

---

in the typescript when "thank" is obviously intended. For example, "thank" in the last sentence of this paragraph was "think" in the Mwase typescript.

4. Conservation laws of all kinds bedeviled Nyasas throughout the colonial regime. They occasioned verbal protest during the 1920's and 1930's; during the 1950's their enforcement helped to provoke violence. Africans particularly disliked prohibitions against the felling of trees along the banks of streams and in catchment areas generally. Soil conservation requirements irked many. The independent Government of Malawi suspended the enforcement of such laws.

of this country understand it or agree with the construing. A native is stopped from cutting a Mbawa, Mlombwa, Msuko, Muwanga, Muula[5] and nearly all trees which would help him for building a stronger house for living in. That means that he is stopped from building stronger homes, stronger "Nkokwe" ⟨granaries, or storehouses generally⟩ and strong cattle kraals. The tree which are prohibited to the native are the only trees to help him all round. They often ask why his law is so strict. The reply they receive is that it is to preserve the trees for your future offspring's use. Natives are put to prison for cutting a muwanga tree for his "nkokwe" or fined heavily for it. They suffer greatly for this respect. Why? If the trees are prohibited for preservation of their future children why should they not have a share for themselves? How the future children may be [more] highly estimated upon, than the parents or primogenitors? Without progenitors how the offspring will be brought out? It was better to allow progenitors to use the trees for their safety and only teach them or tell them about the philoprogenitiveness. And how the worse the future will be if they are cutting and spoiling the trees without use with them. But to stop them entirely from cutting and also punishing them for cutting, that lead them to disbelieve the word "preservation of trees for your future offspring." No native in this country addicts to believe that the preservation of these prohibited trees are for the future offspring. Does not matter educated or uneducated, native is of one form of opinion, that the prohibition of cutting

5. None of these common trees have Western equivalents. Mlombwa is classified as *Pterocarpus angolenis* and Muula as *Parinarum mobola*.

trees for our use by the whiteman's law does not apply
to our children's benefit at all, but it is applying to their
own benefit, and for the benefit of their (whiteman's)
own offspring.

There is no clear reason for native to believe that
only his children will be estimated of much value for
keeping them or preserving for them some kind of
property, which property the father is punished severely when touched it. That sounds quite absurd.
How one could possibly say that I ⟨he⟩ come to protect your food gardens from being spoiled or eaten
by swines because he did not like to see my children
die with hunger in the future, yet he does not allow
me to get some food from the garden to keep me
living and produce the offspring who will use the remainder of the food I was toiled at?[6] What he allows
me to get is only "Mango" (pumpkins)[7] which food
has no longer existence in my stomach and which
is not or stronger food ⟨not a food strong enough?⟩
to empower my veins.

Do you mean to say that I agree with that man
that the food he is preserving for my future offspring?
How he cares only the lives of the future children,
which children he has not seen, and how he expect
me to live and then produce children while prohibited
from eating the food which would make me grow strong-

6. Very likely Mwase meant to start a new sentence at "who
will use," but two interpretations are possible.
7. The word "pumpkins," like all other words in parentheses
( ), appears in the Mwase typescript. *Mango* is not the word
for pumpkin; *mang'a* means cassava; but "pumpkins" here may
be meant as an addition rather than a translation. The author
refers elsewhere to the fruit of the mango tree. Since it provided
important nutritive value in times of seasonal famine, district commissioners encouraged Africans to plant it, and, unlike other trees,
it was never subject to restrictions imposed by the Forestry De-
partment.

er and produce the children? What kind of civility such a person has which is only kept for my future children and he tends ⟨treats⟩ me with inclemency?

The trees which are today prohibited by the whiteman's law are those planted by the Heavenly power, some millions centuries past. Our progenitors used them as much they wanted them, they were never lessen nor diminished. We also used them as much as we wanted them but never reduced their growing until a whiteman found them as many as they were.

The punishments inflicting upon natives heavily for cutting trees discourage them not to be keen in accepting the whiteman's seed for planting trees. Certainly a native receives the seed for planting trees reluctantly from a whiteman, his notion regard the tree which [grows from] seed received from a whiteman is very deep.[8] He thinks that the giving of seed by a whiteman to him is a way to ensnare him, so that he must get a major punishment if the tree is grown which seed was from a whiteman and if that tree is cut either by him or one of his people. He enters into a discourse with another friend of his and reach to a certain conclusion that if I accept the seed I accept nothing else but a very serious trouble on my self and my people, if that tree will be cut afterwards. He adds, if I am punished severely for cutting a tree which the seed and planting is of the sky, and which the whiteman has found it already grown up, which tree no person has laboured for its growing, so what will happen to me if that tree will be cut after it is grown, which seed is from a whiteman, he laboured by carrying his seed from his home, which

8. The forestry services of Nyasaland customarily distributed seed and seedlings to indigenous farmers.

home is very far, he correct ⟨collect?⟩ it all the way
and has again laboured in making nurseries, sowing
the seed, watering it etc.

Yes, he ⟨the African⟩ sees other few people who
planted trees earlier are making use of them, by
themselves, yet he has some doubts. They ⟨the two
Africans⟩ fraternally speak, and fall in a short debate
which brings them a last conclusion that this encouragement of planting trees is followed with great danger after all, does not matter [if] our friends who planted
the trees earlier are having the use of them. Tho'
⟨Nevertheless it⟩ will happen in the same way it happened at the beginning when this law of prohibiting
cutting of trees only applied some few kind of trees,
while the rest were not prohibited. They think this
favour of permitting these people to cut the trees
they have planted, which seed from a whiteman, is
only the way that the majority may be attracted by
it, and adduce themselves to planting them also. When
they all plant and trees grow, then [they may] put the
same restriction from cutting, same as it is applied
to God's planted trees. For instant, these trees are
prohibited at present to all natives, including their
young ones—I mean the young children—but they are
preserved for future children whose children no one
knows from whose they are to belong and who are
going to produce the so expected children, who will
be the heirs of the trees preserved.

I quite agree with demarcation of a Forest Reserve.
The Forest Reserve remind [me of] the primitive way
of reserving a forest for spirits. This reserving of a
forest by the primeval[9] was applied to a certain por-

9. "For the primeval spirits"? In the typescript the word appears as "primeral" here and in the next three instances—then
once as "primeval."

tion of ground which they selected for the purpose
of worshiping "Leza," "Mphambe," "Namchenga,"
"Chauta," [10] at which place they worshiped by burning sacrifices to their "Chauta," so [in] such a place
[one] was prohibited from cutting its trees or burning
the grass thereon. This was called "Nkhalango ya azimu"
or "Nkhalango ya mizimu." [11] Second demarcation of
reserve by primeval was about the patch which was laid
or pointed out for the purpose of burying the deads,
and was called "kudzinja" (Cemetery). [12] Therefore these
two forests only were prohibited to anybody to cut
any trees or burn the grass thereto. If one was found or
accused to either of the offences, such a person was to
be punished by making him or her to pay a fine in kind
and was then warned not to do the foolish actions again
in case the "mizimu" will be angry with him or her
and inflict a heavy punishment by killing or make
him or her go mad.

This primeval demarcation of "Mizimu" Forest was
for the benefit of the parents, children and the future
children, to worship these and for their sacrifices as
well, and the other forest which was called "Dzinja"
was also for the benefit of the parents, children and
the future children for burying their deads. These
forests of the primeval did not make people feel inconvenient about them, because all understood the
purpose of so prohibiting to cut or burn the grass
thereon. They were all of the same mind and thoughts
that such places should be existed. They all understood the use of those forests. So if the whiteman's

10. Various names for God.
11. Thicket of spirits. Mizimu should be spelled *mzimu*. On this
subject, see Thomas Price, "Malawi Rain Cults," *Religion in Africa*
(Edinburgh, 1964, mimeo.), 114–124.
12. More literally, *kudzinja* means a deserted place.

law was laid down against cutting trees in the demarcated Forest Reserves only, the case would not stand as one of much difficulty. The difficulty is due to the diffusion of its law towards all the trees over all the country and all the forests. The prohibition of cutting trees off on the mountains and hills and even near the streams sounds quite well, as it is said that the trees on the mountains and hills help to draw the rains down,[13] and that the trees near the rivers and streams keeps off the dryness of water therein. That is quite consisted ⟨consistent⟩. But what about prohibiting cutting trees which are grown on level places, which places are not at all demarcated or published as Forest Reserves? What is the real aim for this law to prohibit these trees to be cut by natives? I quite agree with the Reserves, cutting off from a hill and cutting trees grown by the stream or river. I do not feel inconvenient [about] it at all. The prohibition of such is the beneficial to me, to my children, and to the future offspring. Does not matter [if] I do not know much what will happen in the future to the Forest Reserves, but I take it in the same way, I observed the primeval law towards the Nkhalango ya mizimu.

I am certain if a native was allowed to cut trees without hindrance or inflicting deadly punishment on him on the trees cut on level places, which were not demarcated as Forest Reserves, would be the cause to induce him to remember to plant more trees of his (or his future offspring) use. He should think that if I keeping cutting the trees without planting more, where am I to get some, if these finish, because the other places are prohibited by the whiteman's

13. In fact, trees were planted in order to retard erosion.

law and they are published ⟨gazetted⟩ as Forest Reserves. Therefore I must be careful to my cutting and remember to plant some for my future use. Certainly he should rush to a whiteman and get as much seed he could plant, and keep a special trees field for himself. But as I have already given the reason above, he is lounging and lingering and pay no attention to what he is told about planting of trees, because he is not sure of the future use of those trees if planted. And looking at the deadly punishment his fellow had received by the whiteman's law for cutting a tree on a level place which was not at all a forest reserve, he quivers and come to a conclusion cryptically, "There is a great danger in dealing with the trees nowadays." Therefore to plant a tree means planting danger near yourself. Here such a friend has been put to prison for cutting a tree or leaving fined ⟨or a fine has been levied?⟩, the tree he has been punished for was not grown up by anybody or seed from anybody, and what will then happen to me if I plant one from his seed? There is a great misapprehension to the native part with regard this law of cutting and the prohibiting thereon.

It will take centuries for a native of that country ⟨Nyasaland⟩ to follow this law correctly. And his being punished for cutting trees will not give him a wary of the danger of so-doing, because he is quite out of the way to understand why all the trees heavily planted are so strictly prohibited to be cut for the use of building strong houses, and he wonders why he pays prices for the tree cut by him for the purpose of building etc. Unless those trees were from the forest reserve or were cut in the hills or near the streams. But he was asked to pay a price of trees cut for his building from any place. A native being an impecunious person, he suffers greatly for his material for building his house so often, instead of building better and big house he elects a very tiny one. This due to each of timber and poles, and also through . . . . ⟨inability⟩ to meet the price of timber.

It is apparently true that a native of this country was not a person to spoil his tree by cutting them, he did not own a large acre garden. His usual garden was from one acre to three acres wide, and a very big garden was not more than five acres, and that garden must be a chief['s] garden, which contained five acres, an ordinary man could not own a five acres garden, because he had not people to help him hoeing.

Is not clear that whiteman is the person who cuts a lot of trees in the country? He owns big acreage of land and hoe very big area of land. Cut all the trees, dig out the stubs ⟨stumps⟩, and make the land impossible to grow more trees on it. But when I see that a native do to his garden, cut a small patch [and] leave the stubs to grow more trees. And when he sees that the soil is washed out in that garden, he leaves it alone for trees to grow again from the stubs, and cut another small patch for his new garden, leaving the other one grow trees for future use.[14] Therefore a native cannot be accused of making his land barren of trees, I ask my reader to consider it when reading about this subject of prohibiting cutting of trees to natives. If I am wrong to what I have explained in regard the law itself, I ask an apology for such a

14. This is an admirable concise description of the traditional method of shifting cultivation followed by most of the Malawi peoples.

pen error. This is all I have to write about the law of trees.

Now I want to remark something with regard prohibition of killing game and game birds. This law should see its way toward the position ⟨the position of the Africans?⟩. The way this law stands now is very much opposing a native who is clearly an impecunious person, who cannot stand the charge paying the licence to kill game. He has no money to meet the charge. Besides asking him to pay for the game, the law should see that a native means the originally born in the country and that he belongs to nowhere, but in the country where he is. Why should he be asked to pay the licence to kill game in his country of origin? [15] I quite agree with the demarcating of Game Reserve in the same way I agree with the "Mizimu" Forests, although they are called by different names by the whiteman. To stop a native to kill game in his own country, which game are not at all in the Game Reserve, brings great doubts to him to understand what is the meaning of such a law. A native could be allowed to kill any game out of the Game Reserve provided he bring Chadziko ⟨token of loyalty⟩ to the Boma. In the case of an elephant killed, the tusks lying on the ground should be the "Chadziko" (loyalty) to the Boma. "Chadziko" to be brought to the big chief is not a strange law to this country, it is the custom of the ancestors, no one would feel inconvenient about that.[16]

This also applies to the rent paid by a native for

15. During this period, the various Nyasa native associations echoed Mwase's refrain with regard to license fees.

16. Traditionally, chiefs had received the ground tusk, i.e., the tusk on which the elephant fell, both as a token of loyalty and as a form of tribute. See also note 4, page 61.

building a business house on a place he thinks suitable for that purpose. He is asked to pay as big rent as an alien pays. This draws away the mind of a native to believe that he is an origin person of the country. He pays it, of course, but with a great murmuring. I remember I went into a discourse with one of the important official of the country about this matter, who seemed to agree with me on the first point, but afterwards checked it out in another sense.[17]

I ask my reader to consider the situation while reading these subjects. Will he not understand my aim? Mind you, my reader, I am not withstand the law at all, but I am explaining out the portion where it has some haven ⟨havoc?⟩ on the part of natives. As I have already said that natives bear the interpretation of people originally born out of the country, or the right people of that particular country or land.[18] So native or to say "natives" has [a more] important meaning, than that to say "Alien," so as the sounds differ [from] each other, the privileges on land should also differ, "Native" bearing the meaning as a person with birth rights on the land, while alien bears the meaning as a person, who has his own land of origin somewhere I do not know, and has come in for a strange interest, either for the interest of thrifty or any other interest.[19] I am not against him for looking after his own interest in the country, and I do not blame him for so-doing. But what I see is that the interest of a native is very much opposed to. He is

17. Mwase had once owned a store on a leased plot near Lilongwe, where he went bankrupt.

18. "The right people" refers to the autochthonous inhabitants.

19. Independent African governments later used this argument, or a variation on the same theme, to restrict rights to the ownership of land.

blamed and punished severely for looking after his own interest which interest has no harm to the public. This great interference to the native interest means nothing else but big mistakes, which mistakes require adjustments.

This country has well known poetry, which reads as follows: "Uchembere ndi kudyelana" ⟨one who has borne children who eat in common⟩. This riddle has a very deep meaning, and has many interpretations. One short interpretation says the love of socialists is the door to handle food together. Secondly bears the meaning that selfishness cuts the love between the communists and many other meanings such as "pity to one, who has sympathy on you, love one, who will return love to you, and help one, who will fall ⟨come⟩ to your help." [20] This riddle is all over in this country, it is in use by nearly all the tribesmen of the country. It existed for centuries. This clearly means that a native is the only person who cries for help and sympathy on his interest, he is a wretched person and impecunious creature on the face of the earth. Therefore to ask him a price for cutting trees, killing game, is indeed, absurd! and punishing him for such is, indeed, unmerciful action! Look at him! and estimate him! surely he does not value anything at present moment in the eye of a great man. Yet the poor creature is asked to pay for anything cut, kill etc.!!

The other remainder of the whiteman's laws are heartily welcomed to, and gratified upon.

Should it be my opportunity, in the future, come across another event which requires observation, will

20. Mwase uses the terms "socialist" and "communist" in a non-political sense.

be apt in recording the same for the public interest, as long it does not harm anybody. I may then give those that desire the hearing of it, an account of what I here am silent about, meantime, I bid my Reader Adieu.

The end.

INDEX

Note: Nyasaland and George S. Mwase are referred to throughout the book and are accordingly not indexed separately. Bantu proper names are indexed without reference to pronominal concords.

Index